BOYHOOD ON

It would be a mistake to whitewash Sam Clemens' gang the way they whitewashed the fence. They were not a band of little angels—in fact few boy gangs are. But they did not fight with knives or guns. They fought mock battles with lath swords, or, in a more serious or desperate mood, fought with their fists. They "hooked" apples and peaches and watermelons, particularly if this forbidden fruit was carefully guarded by slave patrols and dogs, thus making the raid a real adventure. They used any boat that was handy to cross to the island, or to the pecan groves on the Illinois bottoms, or downriver to the cave. But they returned the boats when they had served their purpose.

They were busy with other small deviltries most of the time. But they had their own code of honor and never "snitched" on each other, or let a comrade down in any way. And although they may have seemed in league against the adult world, they were pure of heart and dauntless—very fine pirates and members of Robin Hood's peerless band.

READ THESE OTHER GREAT BOOKS
BY STERLING NORTH:

Rascal
The Wolfling
Young Thomas Edison

MARK TWAIN
AND THE RIVER

STERLING NORTH

PUFFIN BOOKS

PUFFIN BOOKS
Published by the Penguin Group
Penguin Young Readers Group,
345 Hudson Street, New York, New York 10014, U.S.A.
Penguin Group (Canada), 90 Eglinton Avenue East, Suite 700, Toronto, Ontario,
Canada M4P 2Y3 (a division of Pearson Penguin Canada Inc.)
Penguin Books Ltd, 80 Strand, London WC2R 0RL, England
Penguin Ireland, 25 St Stephen's Green, Dublin 2, Ireland
(a division of Penguin Books Ltd)
Penguin Group (Australia), 250 Camberwell Road, Camberwell, Victoria 3124,
Australia (a division of Pearson Australia Group Pty Ltd)
Penguin Books India Pvt Ltd, 11 Community Centre, Panchsheel Park,
New Delhi - 110 017, India
Penguin Group (NZ), 67 Apollo Drive, Rosedale, North Shore 0632,
Auckland, New Zealand (a division of Pearson New Zealand Ltd.)
Penguin Books (South Africa) (Pty) Ltd, 24 Sturdee Avenue, Rosebank,
Johannesburg 2196, South Africa

Registered Offices: Penguin Books Ltd, 80 Strand, London WC2R 0RL, England

First published in the United States of America by Houghton Mifflin Company Boston,
The Riverside Press Cambridge, 1961
Published by Puffin Books, a division of Penguin Young Readers Group, 2009

1 3 5 7 9 10 8 6 4 2

Copyright © Sterling North, 1961
All rights reserved

THE LIBRARY OF CONGRESS CATALOG CARD NUMBER: 61-5138

Puffin Books ISBN 978-0-14-241235-0

Printed in the United States of America

For my wife Gladys, companion and collaborator
for thirty-four creative years.
And also for my brother John Herschel North
and his wife Bess, longtime residents
of Mark Twain's hometown.

My deepest thanks are due to Harper and Brothers for permission to use quotations from several of Mark Twain's books: *The Adventures of Tom Sawyer*; *The Adventures of Huckleberry Finn*; *Life on the Mississippi*; *The Innocents Abroad*; *Roughing It*; and the *Autobiography*.

Years of reading and thinking have been condensed into this little biography of our greatest and most beloved humorist. More than one hundred books and manuscripts by and about Mark Twain have been consulted. The most useful have been: *Mark Twain, the Personal and Literary Life of Samuel Langhorne Clemens* (three volumes) by Albert Bigelow Paine; *Mark Twain's America* by Bernard DeVoto; *Mark Twain, Son of Missouri* by

Minnie M. Brashear, and *Samuel Clemens of Hannibal* by Dixon Wecter.

In addition, many trips have been made to all the Mark Twain shrines, particularly to Hannibal, Missouri, where the cave, the island and the little white house on Hill Street help to re-create the mood in which Twain wrote several American classics.

May I urge every reader to visit the Mark Twain mansion in Hartford, Connecticut; the graves in Elmira, New York, and the octagon summer study on nearby Quarry Farm, but particularly that little city, Hannibal, Missouri, where Mark Twain's spirit still broods over the magnificent, the mile-wide Mississippi.

S. N.

CONTENTS

A WORD ABOUT NAMES

The subject of this biography, known to the world as Mark Twain, was born Samuel Langhorne Clemens, and throughout his entire life was always called "Sam" by his best and oldest friends. He adopted the writing name Mark Twain on February 2, 1863, when he was a reporter on the Enterprise *in Virginia City, Nevada. Throughout this book the names Samuel Clemens and Mark Twain are used almost interchangeably, and of course always refer to the same person.*

A FRONTIER PARADISE
(1835–1844)

Uncle John Quarles stepped down from his farm wagon and tied his team to the hitching post in front of the modest frame house on Hill Street. He noticed that the new home had been given a coat of white paint, and that the shutters on the five front windows were a gleaming dark green. Even the fence had a fresh coat of whitewash.

Quarles smiled with pleasure. His brother-in-law "Judge" Clemens, that proud but unsuccessful tradesman and lawyer, was apparently beginning to pull himself out of debt.

Uncle John wondered which of her children Jane Clemens had dragooned into whitewashing that fence. Certainly not the oldest son, Orion, who at eighteen spent most of his time in St. Louis learning the printing trade. Pamela at sixteen was a gentle young lady with musical inclinations—and no young lady in Hannibal, Missouri, in the year 1844 would be asked to sully her hands with a job like whitewashing a fence. Henry at six was a very good boy, but too young for such a task. So it must have been that rascal Sam, whose eight and a half years had been crammed with more mischief than useful labor. Uncle John liked Sammy the best of all, with his "ruck" of russet curls and his merry blue-green eyes, the delight and despair of his sprightly mother, Jane.

John Quarles had come to Hannibal on the previous afternoon. Not wishing to crowd the little Clemens home, he had spent the night at a neighboring hotel. Now that he had made his purchases, he was ready to pick up Jane and Sam for their summerlong holiday at the big Quarles farm near Florida, Missouri. Aunt "Patsy" Quarles was Jane's sister, and throughout the summer they buzzed away at each other, happy as bees in clover.

For a moment Uncle John paused to view the little white town of Hannibal, bathed in the misty sunlight of this June morning. The village lay cupped in a valley between bluffs to the north and the south. All its attention was centered on the mighty Mississippi, which carried, on its flowing tide, rafts of white pine lumber, handsome side-wheel steamers, painted and gilded; and in flood times masses of floating driftwood and even cabins washed from their foundations. This brown and swirling highway to distant New Orleans captured the imagination of any man who looked upon it—a dangerous river, a beautiful river draining most of the American continent. John Quarles did not wonder that his nephew, little Sammy Clemens, and all the other barefooted boys of Hannibal, were constantly risking their lives in or on its waters.

It would be a long, dusty drive, that thirty-five winding miles to the farm, and this day looked as though it might be another sizzler; so Uncle John turned his gaze from the river to the front door of the house, open for summer coolness, and garlanded on the step with several drowsing cats.

"Jane!" he boomed heartily. "Sam! . . . Where is everybody? Time to get going!"

Sam Clemens, sitting comfortably between his mother and his uncle John on the wide seat of the farm wagon, watched the team of dapple-grays flicking flies with their tails as they ambled easily along the road. He didn't know whether to be happy as a meadow lark or sad as a whippoorwill as the wheels rumbled along the rutted trail leading westward from Hannibal.

It was one of those almost impossible choices which a boy must always be making, such as whether to play Robin Hood or whether to play Pirate; whether to let your warts grow, or whether to risk your life trying to cure them with spunk-water to be found in old hollow stumps in the middle of haunted woods at midnight during the dark of the moon.

Every summer he had to make the same difficult decision about his vacation: whether to stay in Hannibal with Pamela and Henry, and his father the "Judge"—or go with his mother to the Quarles farm. It was always hard to say good-bye to his best friends, Will Bowen, John Briggs, and that happy-go-lucky vagabond, Tom Blankenship, who never had to go to school, and who spent a perfectly heavenly life sleeping in barrels, smoking a corncob pipe, and doing anything else he pleased. But the farm was a gay and joyous place too.

Back in Hannibal he could always go swimming in Bear Creek and risk getting drowned for the ninth

time, or fish catfish, or visit the big cave, which went
forever and ever in mysterious passages. But at the
farm there was at least a cool creek to wade in and
swings that went so high in the air that a tumble
sometimes meant a broken bone. That was almost
as exciting as nearly getting drowned.

There were girls, of course, at both places: little
Laura Hawkins, his best girl, lived just across the
street in Hannibal; once he had given her his finest
possession, a shining brass knob from the top of an
andiron. But she would probably wait for him faithfully until he returned in the autumn. At the farm
was his gay little cousin, Tabitha Quarles, answering
to the name of "Puss." Sam wasn't in love with Puss,
he just liked her, and they had happy and silly times
together. In a way that was much more comfortable
than being in love. So in the girl department, the two
places just about balanced off.

Girls, however, mattered only part of the time.
Boy companions and the storytelling slaves were
what made things lively; and there were plenty of
each at both places. In fact there were eight cousins
and more than twenty slaves at the Quarles farm,
making life as wonderful there as it was in Hannibal.

It was probably the delicious meals Aunt Patsy always served which tipped the scales in favor of another summer at the farm: "Fried chicken, roast pig; wild and tame turkeys, ducks and geese; venison just killed; squirrels, rabbits, pheasants, partridges, prairie chickens; biscuits, hot batter cakes, hot wheat bread, hot rolls, hot corn pone; fresh corn boiled on the ear, succotash, butter beans . . . watermelons, muskmelons, cantaloupes—all fresh from the garden; apple pie, peach pie, pumpkin pie, apple dumplings . . ." Sam couldn't even remember all the rest, but it made him "mouth-watering hungry" just to think of all that good food.

Yes, going to the farm again this summer was an excellent idea, Sam Clemens finally decided as they wound westward and ever westward through the hills of Missouri on that June morning so long ago.

Westward and ever westward might have been the marching cry of the entire nation during the nineteenth century. Like hundreds of thousands of other pioneers, Sam Clemens' father and mother had felt that urge early and often.

John Marshall Clemens, who came of Virginia stock, was reared in Kentucky. Fatherless from the age of seven, and entirely self-supporting from his fourteenth year, he studied for the law, and, being a young man of "honesty, probity and good demeanor," was soon licensed to practice. Although he had worked hard with his hands during his youth, and throughout life was haunted by fear of poverty, he considered himself quite rightly a gentleman and a scholar. He was proud, just, austere, idealistic, dyspeptic, and so lacking in outward signs of affection that Sam never saw him kiss wife or child, save in the presence of death.

Two more strikingly different people than Sam's father and mother could scarcely be imagined.

Jane Lampton (Clemens), whom John married in Columbia, Kentucky, on May 6th, 1823, was one of the most beautiful young women of her region and era. Her oldest son, Orion, wrote of her vivacity and charm. "To the last she retained her rosy cheeks and fine complexion. She took part in the custom in Kentucky and Tennessee, of going on horseback from house to house during the week from Christmas to New Year. To the music of one or two violins they danced all night, slept a little, ate breakfast, and danced all day at the next house . . . Even in the last year of her life she liked to show a company the beautiful step and graceful movement she had learned in her youth." She had a tart tongue but a tender heart.

There was a rumor, never quite denied by Jane, that she married John Marshall Clemens on the re-bound, having been jilted by a young doctor she deeply loved. Be that as it may, she was always a good and faithful wife to her lawyer husband, carrying her heavy load cheerfully through many years of poverty. She guided her children with humor, love and flashes of temper, but always with far greater understanding than that showed by her unbending husband.

Sam respected his father; but he loved his mother, whose temperament was so like his own, and from whom he inherited his wit, his high spirits and his russet curls.

From Kentucky, John Marshall Clemens and his young wife Jane soon moved to Tennessee. They must have made a striking pair—John with his erect posture, his piercing eyes and well-cut features—tall, spare, wearing a blue swallow-tail coat with brass buttons, and the high silk hat expected of a lawyer; Jane young and lovely, with a mischievous tongue and laughing blue-gray eyes and a mass of auburn hair with gold glinting in the curls.

In the wilderness settlements on the upper reaches of the Cumberland River they were considered "Quality" by the log-cabin dwellers because, among other high-flown notions, they insisted upon plastering the inside of their new house. For a time John seemed to be prospering. As acting Attorney General he drew up plans for improving the state in a flawless "copper plate script." At about this time he purchased for the small sum of $400 seventy-five thousand acres of wild, hilly, infertile, forested Tennessee land. This was to be the legacy, the riches for coming generations. It was a rosy-tinted dream that sustained the family during years of poverty—but a dream that never came true. Hold the land! Never let it go! And the Clemens family did hold the land for a generation and a half. But Tennessee was developed so slowly, and the land was so rough and infertile, that when the vast estate slipped from their hands it brought them little more than John Marshall Clemens had paid for it so many years before.

John and Jane moved several times in Tennessee, and always downhill. Poverty came—and then greater poverty. And with the poverty came the children. First there was Orion (which they mispronounced Oh'-rean). This first-born son, who would always have stars in his eyes, and his head in the clouds, came in 1825. He was named for the most conspicuous constellation in the midnight sky—for there was always a touch of poetry in the hearts of John and Jane Clemens.

Next in line was gentle Pamela, born in 1827. She loved music from earliest childhood and would one day play the piano and the guitar. She was never any trouble to her parents and was always her father's favorite child. Years later when he lay dying he asked to kiss but one member of the family—his beloved Pamela.

Third to use the cradle was a rosy little girl named Margaret, most beautiful of all the Clemens children. She arrived with the redbud and dogwood blossoms in May, 1830.

There was a little boy named Pleasants Hannibal, who lived just three months, and then came Benjamin, last of the Tennessee children, born in June, 1832.

They were *wanted* children, loved by the mother, gently treated by the father. But how were the Clemenses to feed so many hungry mouths? John and Jane realized that they must again make a move, this time to some more prosperous region.

As though in answer to their unspoken desire for greener pastures, letters now began to arrive from a frontier settlement called Florida, Missouri—letters praising the fertile limestone soil, the towering hardwood timber, the excellent water and the abundance of game in this unspoiled region. One great attraction for Jane was the fact that so many of her Kentucky kinfolk had already moved to this Missouri village. From her sister Patsy Quarles and Patsy's husband John came affectionate letters urging the Clemenses to pull up stakes and hurry west. Soon this cluster of cabins would be a large and prospering town—or so they all fondly believed. Jane's favorite cousin, James Lampton, went so far as to claim that the shallow Salt River could be deepened and improved until the largest steamboats on the Mississippi could ascend that winding rivulet to deposit passengers and cargo at their very door.*

In the late spring of 1835, John and Jane Clemens

---

*James Lampton, always aglow with "blazing enthusiasm," was the original from whom Mark Twain portrayed his fascinating character Colonel Sellers in *The Gilded Age*. There is a vivid description in that novel of just such a family as the Clemenses moving from the hills of Tennessee to a similar frontier village in Missouri.

and their four living children, Orion, Pamela, Margaret, and Benjamin, loaded their meager possessions into a wagon and began their long journey to Florida, Missouri. Orion, and their one slave, a girl named Jennie, rode horseback. The rest of the family crowded into the wagon. With a sense of high adventure and new hope they clucked to the horses and joined the great westward movement. Somewhere along the way Jane Clemens discovered that she would bear yet another child. She could not know that the new life stirring within her was a baby who would become America's most famous and best-loved humorist. But she did know that this one, like the others, would be welcomed and suckled, loved and chided. And she had the bright hope that this newest arrival when it came into the world would have a better chance to live and thrive in the promised land toward which they were journeying.

As they arrived, dusty and travel-weary, their first view of Florida was dismaying. Could this straggle of log cabins and clapboard shacks be the future metropolis of which they had been dreaming? And could this tiny river be the waterway that was to lure steamships from the Mississippi?

Most of their disappointment, however, was swept away by the warm and joyous reception. Dogs and children, men and women poured from every cabin. Big John Quarles and his lively wife Patsy let their store "keep itself" while they hurried into the road to greet their relatives. John, looking like a frontier scout in his Southwestern haircut, boomed his hearty welcome. Jane and Patsy, those loving and long-separated sisters, embraced tearfully.

Almost before they could wash the dust from their faces, Quarles was offering his brother-in-law, Clemens, a partnership in the store. Money! What did money matter? There would be trade enough to support both families. And only a few doors away stood a two-room clapboard house that would at least shelter them from the weather. As they pulled up their chairs to the ample meal, Jane Clemens thought to herself that they had indeed reached the promised land.

This glow of hope continued for several months, perhaps deep into the autumn of 1835. In November a mysterious stranger from outer space swam into the midnight sky, a heavenly body more brilliant than any star, trailing a train of fiery glory behind it. This was Halley's comet, which was not due to return again for seventy-five years. Surely this comet heralded some great event. And indeed on November 30th a brilliant child was born to Jane, a small, frail, redheaded baby named Samuel Langhorne Clemens, who was to become famous throughout the world.

Mark Twain liked to boast that he had increased the population of Florida, Missouri, by one per cent and could have done as much for London if he had tried. The "almost invisible" town into which he had been born had two streets, paved with dust in summer and with mud the rest of the year. There were twenty-three cabins, and a log church with a puncheon floor under which the pigs rooted, fought, and squealed until it was hard to hear the sermon— supposing a little boy really wanted to hear a sermon instead of enjoying the hog fight underneath the church!

Almost as soon as he could walk, little Sammy found his way to the store kept by his father and his uncle John. It was a very small establishment with "a few rolls of 'bit' calicoes on half a dozen shelves;

a few barrels of salt mackerel, coffee and New Orleans sugar behind the counter; stacks of brooms, shovels, axes, hoes, rakes and such things here and there; a lot of cheap hats, bonnets and tinware strung on strings and suspended from the walls; and at the other end of the room . . . another counter with bags of shot . . . a cheese or two and a keg of powder; in front of it a row of nail kegs and a few pigs of lead, and behind it a barrel or two of New Orleans molasses and native corn whisky on tap."

Sam, who had a sweet tooth, and who many a time was rapped with a thimble for raiding the sugar bowl, would always remember with joy the abundance of sugar at the store. If a boy bought any trifle he was entitled to "half a handful" of sugar, just as any man who bought an axe or a hoe was at liberty "to draw and swallow as big a drink of whisky as he wanted."

It was a somewhat free-and-easy time, a high, wide, and handsome time on the Missouri frontier. Almost everyone was optimistic except those shaking with the fever. Everything was cheap and plentiful—"chickens, ten cents apiece; butter, six cents a pound; eggs, three cents a dozen; coffee and sugar, five cents a pound; whisky, ten cents a gallon."

To be a successful storekeeper in a frontier town, a man had to be friendly, tolerant, sociable and easy-going—but as sharp as a fox. The storekeeper had to laugh at old jokes, wink at the inroads made on his free whisky and crackers, and take eggs in trade for merchandise when no money was available. Jovial Uncle John Quarles was just about perfect for the job (although he never could refuse credit to the poor). But stern, unsmiling John Marshall Clemens lacked every possible characteristic for success in such a business. He continued to be cool, judicious, grammatical and slightly superior to his customers. He disapproved of both drinking and smoking. And he was never known to suffer a fool gladly. To add to his other disqualifications for storekeeping, he was a poor businessman.

It was inevitable that the Quarles establishment would suffer seriously with such a partner, and in time the store "winked out." There was never a moment of hard feeling between these friends. Quarles took his slaves and went to farming. John Clemens began thinking of a new move, this time to the bigger and more prosperous town of Hannibal on the Mississippi.

Before any such move could be made, however, two important events occurred in the Clemens family: a child was born in 1838; and a child died in 1839. The last child born to this marriage was a good and gentle little boy named Henry—the last to use the well-worn cradle. The child who died was the beauty of the family, the rosy-cheeked Margaret —but this tragedy was not yet upon them.

Jane Clemens' fear was not for Margaret during these Florida years. It was Sammy's health that kept her frantic. She dosed him and doctored him with everything from Pain Killer by the spoonful to castor oil by the dipperful. He was a trial and a tribulation to the woman who cared for him.

Once in later years, Sam jokingly asked his mother whether she hadn't feared he might not survive.

"No," said Jane, after a suitable pause, "afraid you would!"

Little Sammy often walked in his sleep, and might be found hours later standing in a corner, cold and miserable, dreaming nightmares, with silent tears running down his cheeks. The first record of such sleepwalking was on a night in August, 1839, when the nearly four-year-old boy made his way in a trance to the foot of his beloved sister Margaret's bed. Sammy no doubt was deeply worried about her serious illness. He stood there in the moonlight, dreaming tragically about her—a bad omen for Margaret, all the slaves said. And the slaves were right, as they so often were on such matters.

Margaret died and they carried her to that high place on the lonely hill where a few gravestones were beginning to gather. You may read that stone today if you wish, half buried in wild roses and black-eyed Susans:

> *Sacred to the Memory*
> *of*
> *Margaret L. Clemens*
> *who died*
> *August 17th–A.D. 1839*
> *In the tenth year*
> *of her age.*

Like so many other gravestones of children it tells nothing of the merry voice now silenced, nor the heartbreak of Mother and Father, sister and brothers. Sammy Clemens, from that day on, found graveyards terrifying places, but fascinating places too.

There was nothing now to hold the family in

Florida, Missouri—that desolate, poverty-stricken little town, doomed from the first to remain a crossroads village. But John Marshall Clemens, after a promising start, was even less successful in Hannibal than he had been in Florida. The family fortunes hit rock bottom in 1842 when Benjamin died, and again in 1843 when "Judge" Clemens was stripped of all his possessions to satisfy creditors. Slowly that poor but honest man was struggling back to solvency as a Justice of the Peace. On a little lot he did not own he had built the house in which the family now lived. Hannibal was a sunny, happy town to barefooted Sam, but to his father it was the scene of additional failures, with storms always threatening the sunshine.

Sometimes Jane Clemens—brave though she always was—thought that in all their restless moving, from Kentucky to Tennessee, from Tennessee to Florida, Missouri, from Florida to Hannibal, they had never caught up with success nor pulled away from their troubles, particularly that grim pursuer, Death. Three small gravestones, like lonesome milestones, marked their winding pathway which led no one knew where. But one thing she did know, she was going to save this little redhead sitting beside her if she had to dose him with all the patent medicines ever concocted.

"A penny for your thoughts," said Uncle John.

"Well, I declare," said Jane, rousing from her reverie and straightening her bonnet, "looks like we're almost to the farm."

The dapple-grays knew that the long day's journey was nearing its conclusion. They whinnied once or twice, turned into the lane without need of guidance, and broke into a fast trot down the home stretch, eager for the oats which awaited them.

Arrival at the Quarles farm was always a gay occasion—nearly as exciting as a circus coming to town. Half a dozen coon dogs came leaping and barking, whining and fawning in an ecstasy of welcome. Cousins appeared from everywhere, tumbled from the haymow, jumped from the swings, or arose from the strawberry patch to shout their greetings. Aunt Patsy came from the house, wiping her hands on her apron. All in one embrace she hugged her sister Jane and her nephew Sammy. Uncle Dan'l, wisest and most admired of all the slaves, stood grinning at the well, forgetful of his task of drawing up the bucket. Sam Clemens would remember it all with nostalgia to the end of his days: "It was a heavenly place for a boy, that farm of my Uncle John's."

The house was a double log one, with a spacious roofed-over area between the two parts—a shaded breezeway where in summer the "sumptuous meals" were served. It stood in the middle of a very large yard enclosed with zigzag rail fences on three sides and tall palings at the rear. Beyond the palings lay the smokehouse where hams and sides of bacon were always being cured with hickory smoke; the orchard, heavy in autumn with apples and peaches; the green and pungent tobacco fields, and, most exciting of all, the slave cabins where lived many good friends, like Uncle Dan'l.

To one side of the house was a wooded hill with hickory, walnut, and ancient oak trees arching high above a clear little brook, "a divine place for wading, and it had swimming pools, too, which were forbidden to us and therefore much frequented by us. For we were little Christian children and had early been taught the value of forbidden fruit."

How long Jane and Sammy extended their visit that summer we do not know. But since they came almost every summer, there must have been occasions when they stayed into the autumn. Mark

Twain in his *Autobiography** recalls vividly the ex-
citements that came after the frost; wild grapes hanging in dusky clusters from the vines of the forest,
hickory nuts lying like a shower of stars under the
trees. As winds grew chill, it was pleasant to gather
around a roaring fire in the family room of the house
"with a trundle bed in one corner and a spinning-
wheel in another—a wheel whose rising and falling
wail, heard from a distance, was the mournfulest of
all sounds to me and made me homesick, and low
spirited and filled the atmosphere with the wandering spirits of the dead; the vast fireplace, piled high
on winter nights with flaming hickory logs from
whose ends a sugary sap bubbled out but did not go
to waste, for we scraped it off and ate it; the lazy cat
spread out on the rough hearthstones; the drowsy
dogs braced against the jambs and blinking; my aunt
in one chimney corner, knitting; my uncle in the

*One of the delights awaiting any reader, young or old, is
Mark Twain's *Autobiography,* written in his maturity and old
age (but for the most part withheld from publication, at his
command, until after his death). Albert Bigelow Paine edited
the first edition of these papers. A better organized selection
was made by Charles Neider—*The Autobiography of Mark
Twain* (Harper and Brothers, 1959).

other smoking his corncob pipe; the slick and car-
petless oak floor faintly mirroring the dancing flame
tongues and freckled with black indentations where
fire coals had popped out and died a leisurely death;
half a dozen children romping in the background
twilight; 'split'-bottomed chairs here and there,
some with rockers; a cradle—out of service but
waiting with confidence; in the early cold mornings
a snuggle of children in shirts and chemises, occupy-
ing the hearthstone and procrastinating—they could
not bear to leave that comfortable place to go out
on the windswept floor space between the house and
the kitchen where the general tin basin stood, and
wash."

As season followed season at the farm, young
Sam Clemens became a stronger, wiser boy—braver
and more adventuresome, and better able to cope
with boyhood life upon his return to Hannibal. Each
year at Uncle John's, his health improved until he
gladly joined the rugged all-night hunts for 'coons
and 'possums, organized on moonlight nights by the
older Quarles boys and the slaves. Stumbling along
behind the eager dogs through the deep shadows of
the mighty forest, they were serenaded by the baying
of the hounds, always pure music to the hunter's ear.

Home were the hunters at sunrise, home from the hill, deliciously tired and famished for a big Missouri breakfast.

Little Sammy now had grown into sturdy Sam Clemens. But there were two deeply ingrained habits he did not quickly outgrow: one was his incorrigible love for minor mischief, and the other his ensuing sense of guilt, which on nights of storm could become sheer terror. Most of his mischief was harmless, such as slipping little garter snakes, or soft little bats, into the closed sewing baskets of Aunt Patsy and his mother. The shrieks which eventually followed seemed well worth the selfless effort. But at night these small misdemeanors grew out of all proportion into sins for which he felt he would never be forgiven. He knew very well from the fiery sermons he had heard that the tortures of Hell awaited bad little boys who wandered happily down the Primrose Path instead of toiling up the Straight and Narrow toward the pearly gates of Heaven. And when lightning flashed across the inky sky, and thunder rolled and boomed, Sam hid his head beneath the covers and asked God to forgive him for his many sins, promising abjectly never to be bad again. At such times he remembered the wild stories told by the slaves of the Devil coming for lost souls on stormy nights, and believed that the whole cannonade was aimed at his own sinful heart. In later years he would confess that like the rest of the human race he was "never quite sane at night."

But when the cheerful sun arose through the tall trees filling the whole world with confidence and joy, Sam forgot his midnight terrors and well-meant promises to be a very good boy. As often as not he would find himself slipping another garter snake into his mother's sewing basket, or even "hooking" a ripe watermelon. In an ecstasy of relief at his reprieve he would whirl until he fell, then roll over and over in the grass, laughing and crying out in sheer animal exuberance. He had forgotten all about the Devil, who but a few hours previously had been gunning for him with bolts of lightning and crashes of thunder.

The superstition, folklore, humor, and wisdom of the slaves did much to shape the thinking of Samuel Langhorne Clemens in those far-off days. Years later he would recall: All the slaves "were friends of ours, and with those of our own age we were in effect comrades."

John and Jane Clemens had owned slaves, usually few in number, since the time of their marriage.

The last of these was Jennie, the slave girl who had ridden horseback on the journey from Tennessee. Like other domestic slaves in Missouri, she was almost a member of the family, and when financial disaster came to the Clemenses in 1843, the sale of this girl was one of the hardest burdens they had to bear. Later they hired for a time, from his owner, a little slave boy named Sandy. "He was from the eastern shore of Maryland," Sam Clemens later recalled, "and had been brought away from his family and his friends halfway across the American continent . . . He was a cheery spirit, innocent and gentle, and the noisiest creature that ever was, perhaps. All day long he was singing, whistling, yelling, whooping, laughing—it was maddening, devastating, unendurable. At last one day, I lost all my temper and went raging to my mother and said Sandy had been singing for an hour without a single break and I couldn't stand it and *wouldn't* she please shut him up. The tears came into her eyes and her lip trembled and she said . . . :

"'Poor thing, when he sings it shows that he is not remembering and that comforts me; but when he is still I am afraid he is thinking and I cannot bear it. He will never see his mother again; if he can sing I must not hinder it, but be thankful for it . . .'

"It was a simple speech and made up of small words, but it went home, and Sandy's noise was not a trouble to me any more."

It is true that during his boyhood days Sam Clemens had no aversion to slavery, because he had never heard a word against it at home, in school, or in church. But even at this early age he was acquiring his strong liking for the race, an appreciation of "certain of its fine qualities."

Twice during his childhood, slaves rescued him from drowning. All the slaves with whom he was acquainted were friendly and entertaining. Sam never forgot the debt he owed the race, and many years later put two Black students through college as a partial payment of that debt.

His most rewarding contact with slaves was at the Quarles farm. They were a well-treated, superior group of bondsmen and his first teachers in the art of dramatic storytelling. Bible stories seemed both pointless and dull in the long-winded sermons Sam heard at church each Sunday. But there was nothing dull from Genesis through Revelations when bright

slaves re-created these pulsing and vivid tales—
Moses leading his people through the Red Sea,
David with his sling facing the mighty Goliath,
Solomon in all his glory; what a pageant of characters, laughing, shouting, slaying and praying, sin-
ning and repenting. They all came fearfully and
beautifully alive through the magic of the storytellers in the slave cabins on the Quarles farm. Here
too Sam heard the plaintive and tender spirituals
which he continued to sing for the rest of his life:

> *Swing low, sweet chariot*
> *Coming for to carry me home . . .*

Most beloved of all was Uncle Dan'l, "a middle-
aged slave whose head was the best . . . whose sympathies were wide and warm and whose heart was
honest and simple and knew no guile." He was the
original from whom Mark Twain drew one of the
greatest characters in American fiction, the runaway
slave Jim, who floated "down the Mississippi and
into immortality" on a raft with Huckleberry Finn.

"I know the look of Uncle Dan'l's kitchen as it
was on the privileged nights, when I was a child, and
I can see the white and black children grouped on

the hearth, with the firelight playing on their faces and the shadows flickering on the walls, clear back toward the cavernous gloom of the rear." On such an autumn night, owls sometimes hooted mournfully in the forest beyond the cabin, and sometimes the howl of a wolf was heard above the crackling of the cozy fire. Then Uncle Dan'l began to tell his deathless tales to the accompaniment of the wind, sighing around the cabin like spirits of the departed. The last story was usually one which gave Sam a quivering "creepy joy"—the ghost story of "The Golden Arm."

Many tongues have shaped this tale over the years. But essentially it tells of a monstrous mean man who lived way out on the prairie all alone by himself, except that he had a wife with a golden arm, all solid gold from the shoulder down.

After a time the wife died, and her husband took and toted her way out on the prairie and buried her in a lonely, secret place. But he was so monstrous mean that he couldn't sleep that night, because he wanted the golden arm so badly.

At midnight, when he could stand it no longer, he took his lantern and pushed out through the storm to dig her up and get her golden arm. He bent his head into the wind and plowed on through the drifting snow until at last he came to the lonely, secret place where she was buried. Then he dug her up, and took the arm, and started back through the blizzard. It was a long way through the stormy night.

Then, all of a sudden, he stopped, and listened. At first all he could hear was the wind, sighing and moaning across the prairie, and around the drifts of snow. Then he heard a voice, mingled with the wind, way back there by the grave: "Who—got—my—golden—arm?"

And he began to shiver and shake and say, "Oh, my! Oh my land!" And just then the wind blew the lantern out, and the snow whipped across his face in such a driving fury that he could scarcely breathe. He tried to run through the knee-deep snow, almost dead with terror, and soon he heard that voice again, mingled with the moaning wind: "Who—got—my—golden—arm?"

When he got to the pasture he heard it again, closer now, and coming, coming, back there in the dark of the storm. When he reached the house he rushed upstairs and jumped into bed, and covered up head and ears and all, and lay there shivering and shaking. And then, way out there, he heard it again, coming, coming.

Then by and by he heard—pat, pat, pat—it was coming up the stairs; then he heard the latch open and knew it was in the room. Then he knew it had moved across the room and was standing by the bed, bending over him, and he could scarcely get his breath. Then, then he seemed to feel something icy cold, right down almost against his head. And then the voice said, plaintively: "Who—got—my—golden—arm?"

A long pause here, while Uncle Dan'l stared straight at Sam Clemens, a breathless pause in that silent circle of joyfully terrified children. Then Uncle Dan'l reached out swiftly with both hands to grab Sam by the shoulders and shout: "You've got it!"

That was the climax of the evening, and now the children must leave the warm safety of that fire-lit cabin and make their way through the darkness to their own beds. Sam would always remember "the bare wooden stairway," the turn to the left at the landing, how the rafters slanted above his bed and the "squares of moonlight on the floor." He would lie awake for perhaps an hour, thinking of his sins and listening, listening for the pat, pat, pat of ghostly footsteps on the stairway, the lifting of the latch, and the voice which might at any moment mingle with the autumn wind, still sighing through the trees.

And so another fruitful season had passed at the farm, and Sammy and his mother were ready to return to Hannibal. The boy who was to become Mark Twain had added yet another cubit to his stature, and yet a further treasure of tales and memories which would one day make him one of the finest storytellers in America. And Uncle Dan'l was a few months nearer to becoming a beloved and unforgettable character in American literature.

2

BOYHOOD ON THE RIVER
(1844–1847)

Looking back on his boyhood, Mark Twain would always remember Hannibal as it was in the mid-1840's: "the white town drowsing in the sunshine of a summer's morning: the streets empty or pretty nearly so; one or two clerks sitting in front of the Water Street stores, with their splint-bottomed chairs tilted back against the walls, chins on breasts, hats slouched over their faces, asleep . . . a sow and a litter of pigs loafing along the sidewalk, doing a good business in watermelon rinds and seeds; two or three lonely little freight piles scattered about the 'levee'; a pile of 'skids' on the slope of the stone-paved wharf, and the fragrant town drunkard asleep in the shadow of them."

A slave town in Missouri, peacefully asleep. But at any moment now the great event of the day would wake it from its slumber, for Hannibal's only contact with the outside world was the traffic of gaudy packets coming upriver from St. Louis or downriver from Keokuk.

Suddenly a film of smoke would appear, far up or down the river. A Black drayman would shout, "S-t-e-a-mboat a-comin'" and instantly the scene would change. "The town drunkard stirs, the clerks wake up, a furious clatter of drays follows . . . all in a twinkling the dead town is alive and moving . . . Drays, carts, men, boys all go hurrying . . . to the wharf."

The boat now maneuvering for a landing is a handsome sight, its tall stacks belching jet-black pitch-pine smoke. In the glass pilot house the lordly pilot in blue coat and white trousers stands at the wheel. The paddle boxes are ablaze with gilded rays surrounding the boat's name. All three decks are "fenced and ornamented with clean white railings; there is a flag gallantly flying from the jack staff; the furnace doors are open and the fires glaring bravely . . . the captain stands by the big bell, calm, imposing," the envy of all the passengers crowding the upper decks, and the audience assembled on the levee.

You may be sure that Sam Clemens and his gang

are there—John Briggs, "The Terror of the Seas," Tom Blankenship, the "Red-Handed," Will Pitts, and probably the two younger Bowen boys. They look upward with reverence at the captain and the pilot. They even envy the deck hands who can follow the river day and night, year after year on this floating palace, gliding all the way to New Orleans, perhaps —to see the great world far down the gleaming river. No wonder it is the "permanent ambition" of every boy in Hannibal to some day become a river pilot. And not a few of these barefooted, one-gallus urchins will eventually have that ambition satisfied. Now for ten wonderful minutes while the boat unloads freight and passengers, these boys may gaze at their dream in all its splendid reality—crystal chandeliers flashing like diamonds in the dim salons, gamblers in crimson vests and high silk hats escorting women twirling their small parasols—but best of all, the pilot in his fanciful pilot house, master of the river in all its many moods. Just think of being at the wheel of a boat like that!

Those would always be the good old times on the Mississippi in Mark Twain's memory—perpetual summer, eternal youth, and "the majestic, the magnificent Mississippi rolling its mile-wide tide along."

John Marshall Clemens, sitting in his shabby little law office on Bird Street, heard the commotion outside his window, the rattle of the drays, the tattoo of running feet pounding on the board sidewalks, the steamboat whistling for a landing and then the clear tone of its bell. He did not glance up from his labor, nor did his hand pause, as his pen continued to shape cool, meticulous legal phrases.

"Judge" Clemens was actually a Justice of the Peace, and his makeshift courtroom was this same law office. His desk was a big dry-goods box, his chair a three-legged stool. Four other such stools, a puncheon bench, and an old lounge constituted the remaining furniture in this bare room. On the dry-goods box rested a big wooden gavel with which he rapped for order during court sessions. On one occasion when a scuffle developed and an old pepperbox revolver had been fired, the judge leaned over his desk and rapped for order with his gavel on the head of the chief offender, who thereupon "sank senseless to the floor." Courteous Virginia gentleman though he was, Judge Clemens could be formidable when dispensing justice.

Now, in the mid-1840's, John Marshall Clemens was still deep in poverty. He was forty-seven years of age, "very tall, very spare, with a long, thin, smooth-shaven intellectual face. The long black hair that lay close to his head, was kept to the rear by his ears . . . and fell straight to his coat collar . . . He had an eagle's beak and an eagle's eye."

That eye saw all and knew all. Or so it seemed to Judge Clemens' nine-year-old son, Sammy, who had reason to believe that his father was the best-educated man in town and nobody to be trifled with. He always spoke precise and proper English, a characteristic he had managed to impose upon his oldest son, Orion, and to some extent upon his beloved daughter Pamela. Sam and his mother drawled along amusingly in unassuming homespun phrases.

The Judge was the president of the Library Institute, which treasured its few books in a little room on the second floor of a building on Wild Cat Corner. Like Orion, Pamela, and even little Henry, the Judge usually had his nose in a book—a pleasurable habit which Sammy had not yet acquired. It astonished and slightly intimidated this barefooted son of his to hear his father speak so knowingly on national politics or on the promising future of the State of Missouri and the town of Hannibal. Judge Clemens could tell you—

That in this year of 1845 steamboats had been on the Mississippi for exactly thirty-four years; that Missouri had been a state since 1821, and Hannibal a village since 1819. He knew the voting margin by which James K. Polk had just been elected President of the United States, and he was now predicting that Polk would lead us into war against Mexico.

John Marshall Clemens was a peaceful man who had taught his children to hate war. But he was also a pro-slavery advocate who had helped to jail three abolitionists. The slave states were more eager for war with Mexico than were the free states to the north. It posed a difficult problem in the mind of this honorable man.

Meanwhile the Judge dreamed of civic improvement. He cast his sharp eye over the rowdy little community about him and yearned to reform the drunkards, jail the criminals, and educate the thoughtless young people who swarmed with joy up Holliday's Hill, through the cave, and out upon the river.

Judge Clemens felt that Hannibal had distinct possibilities. Already it boasted lumber mills and gristmills, two slaughterhouses that killed and dressed 10,000 swine a year, several stores, two hotels, three blacksmith shops, and a tobacco factory. Unfortunately it also had distilleries and at least four saloons which kept such fragrant town drunkards as Woodson Blankenship (father of Tom), "General" Gaines, and Jimmy Finn quite unaware of their troubles—Finn being perfectly happy to sleep it off among the pigs of the abandoned tannery. To somewhat offset this revelry there were two churches, Methodist and Presbyterian, which the Judge never attended, but which he supported from a sense of decorum; and two private schools where Pamela and even little Henry earned the approval of their teachers, but where his mischievous boy Sam was usually on the receiving end of a hickory switch. Judge Clemens shook his head and wondered for the thousandth time why Sam alone among his children actually preferred the society of such utterly illiterate and unwashed boys as Tom Blankenship.

Yes, the town of Hannibal, and even his rascal Sammy, might be redeemed if the Judge worked hard enough and dreamed lofty enough dreams. He wanted more books for the library, an academy for the town, a railroad to St. Joseph, a telegraph wire from the outside world, better streets and macadamized county roads. Even as he struggled, fruitlessly, to pay his debts and support his family, Judge Clemens held his head a little higher, brushed his shabby coat a little more vigorously, and placed his duty to the community first, as he felt a gentleman should. Swindled out of almost all he possessed by such shady local citizens as William Beebe, the slave-trader, and big Ira Stout, the crooked real estate operator, Judge Clemens would not let his high standards of impartial justice deviate by an iota. Ramrod stiff, proud and unsmiling, he now closed his office, locked the door, and started home to Jane and the children in the little house on Hill Street.

John Clemens entered his home to find Pamela perfecting her fingering of "I Wander by the Brookside" —a song she hoped to teach her more advanced students on the guitar. Her small but true voice blended sweetly with the rich chords; and her auburn curls, so like her mother's, caught the glint of the late sunlight falling through the window. She smiled, and for the first time in many days Judge Clemens smiled too.

In the kitchen the Judge found the usual amiable confusion, a clutter of contented cats, a pile of clothes in the corner awaiting washday, and Jane moving nimbly about the stove, turning the catfish frying in the skillet. John and Jane exchanged polite greetings, and the Judge stepped from the back door to find the boys. Sam, as usual, was missing, but little Henry was trying manfully to pull the big, dusty Jimson weeds growing between the rows of beans, beets, and cabbages.

"Hello, Henry," said the Judge, with cool courtesy. "Where is Sam?"

Henry dug his toe in the dust and dropped his eyes. Telling on Sam was becoming a very dangerous pastime. Only a few days before he had been so incautious as to reveal that Sam had played hooky from school and had gone swimming in Bear Creek. His reward for this utter honesty was a good clodding from his redheaded brother.

Henry," his father said sharply, "answer my question!"

Obviously there was no chance for evasion. He sighed and told the truth, the whole truth, and nothing but the truth (which was exactly what Judge Clemens always demanded from any witness). Tom

Blankenship had "meowed" from the other side of the back fence. Sam had stopped pulling Jimson weeds and had gone over the fence to join Tom, John Briggs, and Will Bowen. Henry had trailed them at a safe distance and had seen them "borrow" a rowboat near the ferry landing and start out across the river toward the island. They had taken a frying pan, some bacon, and their fishing lines. So there would be no use waiting supper.

"Bother that boy," said Jane at the kitchen door. "He'll be the death of me yet. But I'm not afeared of his drowning any more. A person born to be hanged is safe in the water."

Jane Clemens, five years her husband's junior, was as different from the Judge as morning is from midnight. If he was an eagle, she was a jenny wren— a small, quick, happy thing. The Judge was orderly, neat and serene. Jane was a happy-go-lucky house-keeper and prone to moments of tenderness and temper. Probably the Judge loved his children and his wife in his own odd, undemonstrative way, but only with Pamela did he ever show a touch of human warmth. Jane loved all her children and showed it, and they in turn loved her. The stern head of the household never played games or joked or proposed a holiday. Jane was always ready for a frolic, and her little feet could never be still when Pamela struck up a lively tune on the guitar. How long it had been since John had joined her in a dance!—and dancing had been her greatest joy when she was a young girl.

Jane was a churchgoer and a connoisseur of funerals. John was a man of highest morals, but he drew the line at churchgoing, and he deplored the Bible-thumping, fire-and-brimstone oratory which passed for religion in most frontier towns. Jane complained gently that he couldn't even enjoy a heart-wringing funeral, with tears and flowers and kind words for the departed. Jane took her religion with a grain of salt, but she took it in large doses every Sunday—and made her children do the same. Sister Clemens had first been a Methodist and was now a Presbyterian. But she might have made half a dozen more changes of faith if there had been more churches in town. She went mostly for the hymn-singing and the sociability; and her minister called her a fine, upstanding member of his congregation.

She had, said her famous son, "a slender, small body, but a large heart—a heart so large that everybody's grief and everybody's joys found welcome in it . . ." No grieving neighbor was ever turned away from her door. No stray cat ever had to "meow" twice for a saucer of milk and a place by the fire. At one time there were nineteen cats in the Clemens' kitchen, and each one loved. Jane tried to keep the cats from catching the mice, because she felt kindly toward mice too—even toward flies that got into the house, despite the cheesecloth at the windows. When at last the cat population was impossibly large, and a litter of new kittens had to be drowned, Jane warmed the water to the temperature of a baby's bath, and, after the awful deed was done, cried in guilt and remorse.

She had given some of her gentleness to all her offspring—and to all of them her love of birds and flowers and trees. Never in their lifetime would any of these children keep a pet in a cage, because Jane had taught them it was cruel. Orion (still learning the printing trade in St. Louis) was so mild-mannered and ineffectual that he found it hard to compete with the ungentle world in which we live. Jane's tenderness permeated the nature of Pamela and Henry. It deeply influenced Sam, who grieved that the leaves died each autumn and who pitied the 'coon or 'possum treed by the dogs in the all-night hunts. Once, when he accidentally dropped a brick on the finger of his best girl, Laura Hawkins, he cried harder than she did over her hurt.

Gentleness they all had, but only to Sam did his mother give her sparkle and spunk, her sardonic wit, and her outspoken truth-telling. "Sammy's long-talk" was another inheritance from his mother, whose Southern drawl was charming and likely to stop all other conversation while the listeners waited for the delayed explosion at the end of almost every sentence.

On the gay side, Jane gossiped, but never with malice; played cards, but never for money; and, while still a good-looking young woman, sometimes smoked a pipe, her eyes dancing their challenge at her husband who deplored smoking as he did all other vices.

On her serious side she was the avowed enemy of all tyranny, and absolutely fearless in berating men who beat their horses or dogs. Samuel Langhorne Clemens, who throughout life was the bitter enemy of oppressors everywhere, learned moral courage from his mother.

"She was the natural ally and friend of the friendless," Sam Clemens would later testify. "Whenever anybody or any creature was being oppressed, the

fears that belonged to her sex and her small stature
retired to the rear and her soldierly qualities came
promptly to the front. One day in our village I saw a
vicious devil . . . a common terror in the town, chasing his grown daughter past cautious male citizens
with a heavy rope in his hand and declaring he
would wear it out on her. My mother spread her
door wide to the refugee and then, instead of closing
and locking it after her, stood in it and stretched her
arms across it, barring the way. The man swore,
cursed, threatened her with his rope; but she did not
flinch or show any sign of fear; she only stood
straight and fine and lashed him, shamed him, de-
rided him, defied him in tones not audible to the
middle of the street but audible to the man's con-
science and dormant manhood; and he asked her
pardon and gave her his rope and said with a most
great and blasphemous oath that she was the bravest
woman he ever saw; and so went his way without
another word and troubled her no more."

With such a mother and father it would have been
strange if Sam had been a really bad boy. But it must
be admitted that he wasn't always a really good boy
either. When he had been swimming against orders,

or had played hooky from school, he often lied about it. But when neighbors came to Jane with accusations against Sammy's veracity, Jane's dander was immediately up. She admitted she discounted ninety per cent of what Sammy told her, but insisted that the other ten per cent was "pure gold." It was Jane's duty to punish Sam (just as Sam felt it was his duty to escape punishment if he possibly could); but she must have spanked him more with love than with righteous anger. It was her deep concern for him and not her fits of temper that often broke Sam's heart. But no matter how often he promised to be good, temptation soon fell in his way—usually within a matter of hours; and he was out the window, down the rainpipe, and off on some new escapade.

Sam Clemens believed that his father "possessed the power of life and death over all men, and could hang anybody who offended him." Only twice in his life was he punished by his father, and then not too severely. But a stern glance from the Judge usually sufficed. Mark Twain wrote in later years, "My father and I were always on the most distant terms when I was a boy—a sort of armed neutrality, so to speak." To offer an idea of how remote and cool

John Marshall Clemens really was, each evening, before going to bed, it was his custom to shake hands, formally, with his wife and his children. Hannibal obviously was not a "kissing community"—particularly in the Clemens household.

Judge Clemens was an upright and an excellent man, doing his duty to family and community. But the shadow of his quiet severity seemed to extend over his son's entire life—making that son rebel against all masculine authority—school, church, or oppressive form of government—during the seventy-five years he was on earth. It seems a great pity that two such fine people never learned to understand each other. But the fact is undeniable: they never did.

Sam had begun his lifelong rebellion early. It seemed, during those boyhood years on the river, that he could never breathe enough of the wild freedom of Holliday's Hill, the cave, the island—the immensity of the sky above him by sunlit day or by starlit night. His mother had taught him that it was cruel to cage a bird, and in her heart she must have known she could not cage Sammy either.

Nobody was sure that Sammy ever *could* be tamed in those early years. But the love of his mother, his sister, and the little girl across the way had some effect upon him. It was for Laura Hawkins* that he showed off in school and Sunday school, on the playground and in the street. She was "a lovely little blue-eyed creature with yellow hair plaited into two long tails, white summer frock and embroidered pantalettes." But she wasn't as easy to win as Sam had thought she might be. He tried just about every way he knew to gain her love, such as pushing other boys, sharing his candy with her, carrying her schoolbooks, and giving her the brass knob we have mentioned. He even took a whipping for her in school. But misunderstandings were always threatening

---

*As Mark Twain has admitted, many of the events in *The Adventures of Tom Sawyer* really occurred, and almost all the characters are drawn in whole or in part from real life. Becky Thatcher is Laura Hawkins, Tom Sawyer is largely a self-portrait of Sam Clemens. His mother posed for Aunt Polly, just as Pamela Clemens furnished the amiable outlines for Mary. Sam's younger brother Henry, who was actually a much finer boy, is caricatured in the book as Sid Sawyer. Tom Blankenship, who lived just over the back fence, is the immortal Huckleberry Finn, who "slept on doorsteps in fine weather and in empty hogsheads in wet." John Briggs was the real, flesh-

their stormy courtship in the early months. Sam sometimes walked desolate and alone, thinking how sad Laura would be if he should ever be drowned.

But girls could not share most of the boy pleasures of Hannibal. They couldn't go swimming and fishing with the boys on the island. They were useless when digging for gold or playing pirate. And they seemed to be oddly scornful of such treasures as broken Barlow knives, marbles, half-eaten apples, or a dead rat to swing on a string—the sort of priceless tribute one could get from friends for allowing them to whitewash your fence for you. In fact, girls were mostly in the way no matter how much you loved them.

It would be a mistake to whitewash Sam Clemens' gang the way they whitewashed the fence. They were not a band of little angels—in fact few boy gangs are. But they did not fight with knives nor

and-blood version of Joe Harper, "The Terror of the Seas." And while it is true that the boys, for all their treasure hunting, never found "a little over twelve thousand dollars," *Tom Sawyer* is essentially an honest picture of life in and around Hannibal, Missouri, in the 1840's. It is a poem to youth which will endure as long as there are young readers and as long as the magnificent Mississippi continues to pour its waters southward toward the Gulf.

guns. They fought mock battles with lath swords, or, in a more serious or desperate mood, fought with their fists. They "hooked" apples and peaches and watermelons, particularly if this forbidden fruit was carefully guarded by slave patrols and dogs, thus making the raid a real adventure. They used any boat that was handy to cross to the island, or to the pecan groves on the Illinois bottoms, or downriver to the cave. But they returned the boats when they had served their purpose.

They were busy with other small deviltries most of the time. But they had their own code of honor and never "snitched" on each other, or let a comrade down in any way. And although they may have seemed in league against the adult world, they were pure of heart and dauntless—very fine pirates and members of Robin Hood's peerless band. They were, in short, ordinary smalltown boys with a playground as big as the whole outdoors.

Sam and his friends were genuinely shocked by actual violence when they saw it. The real roughnecks of the town were the Hyde brothers, who had pepperbox revolvers which they liked to shoot into the air as they walked along the streets, scaring the citizens of Hannibal half to death. Once Sam and his friends saw one of the Hyde boys pinning his uncle to the ground while the other villainous brother held his revolver to the old man's head. The hammer clicked, clicked and clicked again without managing to fire a bullet, and so the terrified man was saved from death.

Hannibal was not a frontier town—the real frontier having moved much farther west. Killings were not so commonplace that they were easily forgotten. There were frequent drownings, of course, of small boys trying to swim across to the island, or of passengers who fell from the river boats. But it was not until September 4, 1843, when the town was nearly a quarter of a century old—that the first homicide occurred.

Two drunken farmers named Hudson and McFarland began quarreling over a plow. Hudson stabbed McFarland with an eight-inch knife and the victim soon was dead. This undoubtedly was the corpse, laid out in Judge Clemens' rude little court room, so eerily described by Mark Twain in his book *The Innocents Abroad*:

"I remember yet how I ran off from school once, when I was a boy, and then, pretty late at night, concluded to climb into the window of my father's office and sleep on a lounge, because I had delicacy about going home and getting thrashed. As I lay on the lounge and my eyes grew accustomed to the darkness, I fancied I could see a long, dusky, shapeless thing stretched upon the floor. A cold shiver went through me. I turned my face to the wall. That did not answer. I was afraid that that thing would creep over and seize me in the dark."

Gradually moonlight moved across the floor until it revealed—a white human hand—then slowly, slowly a naked arm, and finally "the pallid face of a man . . . with the corners of the mouth drawn down, and the eyes fixed and glassy in death."

After a few more moments of near paralysis, Sam was suddenly galvanized into action. He says he went through the window without bothering to open it—and perhaps he did.

The murder that most impressed and depressed Sam during these years occurred on January 24, 1845. It was the cold-blooded shooting of old Sam Smarr, an incident which in a different guise is dramatized very effectively in *Huckleberry Finn*. "Uncle Sam" Smarr, a harmless old codger, was very loud and abusive when drunk. He had a grievance, or thought he had, against William Owsley, one of the village merchants, who, having taken all the insults he could tolerate, shot Smarr twice, with great deliberation and at close range, while Smarr's daughter pleaded for the old man's life. As Smarr lay dying, some sanctimonious citizen brought a great family Bible and placed it upon his heaving chest.

Wrote Mark Twain in his *Autobiography*:

"The shooting down of poor old Smarr in the main street at noon-day supplied me with some more dreams; and in them I always saw again the grotesque closing picture—the great family Bible spread open on the profane old man's breast by some thoughtful idiot and rising and sinking to the labored breathings and adding the torture of its leaden weight to the dying struggles."

Slavery, no matter how mild in form, has always been accompanied by some degree of violence. Mark Twain says that cruelties were rare and unpopular between master and slave in Hannibal during his youth. But he did remember the casual killing of one slave for a trifling offense, and he also remembered vividly "a dozen black men and women chained to one another . . . and lying in a group on the pavement, awaiting shipment to the Southern slave market. Those were the saddest faces I have ever seen . . ."

Perhaps the most dramatic slaying that Sam Clemens and John Briggs ever witnessed was that of a "Californian emigrant" who had been shouting taunts and insults at a widow and her daughter who lived in what was known as the "Welshman's House" part-way up Holliday's Hill. The boys arrived in time to hear the widow tell the drunken stranger that she would take no more of it, and would shoot after counting to ten. The young man stopped shouting but stood his ground in surly defiance, and she began to count—one—two—three—four. He did not flinch nor turn away and the angry woman was equally determined. So—five—six—seven—eight—nine. Here there was a longer pause to give the intoxicated brawler one last chance. Then came the fatal count—ten! A terrible flash split the gathering darkness and the man fell mortally wounded. At almost the same moment, thunder rolled across the valley and a great storm broke.

Every man and boy in Hannibal always rushed to the scene of a slaying, and they reacted predictably on this occasion. Sam Clemens would remember them swarming up the hill "in the glare of the light-ning like an invasion of ants."

Storms often seemed to break at times of violence in Sam Clemens' young life. At about this time Injun Joe (who didn't really die of starvation in the cave) came to his obscure death, and all the slaves and young people believed that the Devil would surely come to take the half-breed's soul. Lightning and thunder crashed all night. And Sam, shivering in his bed, prayed long and earnestly, fearing that the Devil, to save time and trouble, might decide to carry a double load back to Hell, taking Sam's soul too. He promised never again to lie, never to play hooky—in short, to turn over a new leaf and to be henceforth the best boy in Hannibal. He "begged like a dog" for forgiveness—if only this once he could be saved from eternal damnation. Rumble, flash, BANG! went the thunder and lightning between the hills and over the great river. At last he fell asleep to dream his usual nightmares.

But by dawn the storm had passed, and the world, newly drenched and clean and green, sparkled as innocently as it must have sparkled in the Garden of Eden. Sam's heart was washed free of sin and all of his night terrors had vanished. It was too beautiful a day to stay in school. He would have to get in touch with John Briggs and Will Bowen and see if they would join him in a jaunt to the island.

Sam learned so little in school and played hooky so frequently that his "formal education" can be covered in a few paragraphs. Apparently he attended classes for seven or eight years beginning at the age of four and one half. He was thrashed the first day and regularly thereafter, and accepted these stinging reprimands with no lasting bitterness, it being the code of the boys to see who could take the hardest beating while doing the least howling. One other form of punishment for milder misdemeanors was to be made to sit on the girls' side of the room, a very sweet form of punishment indeed when Sam could sit beside golden-haired Laura Hawkins.

During these years Sam studied lightly under five teachers: Mrs. Horr, Miss Newcomb, Miss Torrey, Mr. Dawson, and Mr. Cross. At Mrs. Horr's school, where the other two women also taught, Sam learned mathematics to long division, studied spelling from Webster's *Speller* and reading from McGuffey's first three graded *Readers*. He learned how to take off his cap when entering a room, how to say "please" and "thank you," how to rattle off his ABC's and multiplication tables. In later years Sam would admit, "I owe a great deal to Mary Newcomb, she compelled me to learn to read." But in only one subject did Sam Clemens always stand at the head of the class. He never wore the medal for "best deportment" but he always wore the one awarded the best speller. Once he let Laura Hawkins "spell him down" and was very proud to see that medal pinned for a week to her gingham pinafore.

Bible reading, prayers, the recitation of sentimental poetry; and, once each year, the happy May Day celebration!—these constituted the dutiful efforts of the three devoted women struggling to teach Sam Clemens and his friends the fundamentals in that little one-room log schoolhouse at the southern end of Main Street, in Hannibal so long ago.

It was customary in those days for women to teach the younger children, but for men to take over the more difficult task after the third year. The ladies at the dame school must have breathed a long sigh of relief as they passed along Sam Clemens, John Briggs, and the Bowen boys to Mr. Dawson and Mr. Cross. William O. Cross was a middle-aged Irishman who kept school in a little building on the public square facing Center Street. Here Laura Hawkins and Sam's other companions were again the chief attraction, while the poor schoolmaster was the common enemy.

Sam's first recorded literary effort was a two-line poem, which, when written on the blackboard, produced an instantaneous response from his teacher:

Cross by name and cross by nature
Cross jumped over an Irish potato.

How could any of Sam's teachers know, as the heavy switch fell and fell again, that their only immortality would be a mention or two in the future books written by the boy they were beating, or that in due time Yale and even Oxford would tenderly award this same unruly scholar their highest honorary degrees? Of all the children in the room only one had genius—but Sam kept this fact well hidden during his school days in Hannibal.

Cross's school had the same flaw Sam had noticed at Mrs. Horr's. It had windows, and those windows looked out upon the "boy paradise" outside— Holliday's Hill. It was indeed hard to parse dull sentences when one thought of the deep forests where the partridge drummed, the mossy ravines and little creeks of clear cold water, the berry patches hanging with luscious fruit, and the swirling brown, mile-wide river which Sam could now swim across and back without resting—like most of his friends, a seal in the water. Yes, he was learning slowly in school—and perhaps he needed all the book knowledge he could ever get. But he needed other knowledge too—knowledge of where the muskrats had their dens and houses, where the squirrels and raccoons lived in their hollow trees; knowledge of the endless flights of wild geese, wild ducks and passenger pigeons, north in the spring and south in the fall, along this great central flyway of the Mississippi Valley. He must know the oak and hickory and maple; where to find walnuts, pecans, and grapes in heavy clusters. He must know the budding of spring, and the wash of gold and crimson that swept the valley when the frost splashed the billowing forest with autumn colors. School is important for us all; so is life! But it was from his unforgettable experiences on those stolen days that Mark Twain wrote the purest song to boyhood ever to find its way onto a printed page.

To be a full-fledged member of Sam Clemens' gang, a boy had to be brave, romantic, mischievous, and adventuresome, ready at a moment's notice to play Robin Hood, Pirate, or any of the other games which took them up the slope and into the forest, high on Holliday's Hill. It was always easy to round up a few of his closest friends, Will Bowen, John Briggs, and Tom Blankenship, for example. Will and John were slightly younger than Sam, but sturdy, dependable, happy-spirited companions. Tom Blankenship, somewhat older than the other three, was a very special character. He was one of several children of Woodson Blankenship, a ne'er-do-well who drank up what little he earned and let his family struggle along as best it could in the dilapidated barnlike structure, directly behind the Clemens house and facing upon the next street north.

Young Blankenship was always dressed in cast-off clothes. "His hat was a vast ruin with a wide crescent lopped out of its brim . . . he did not have to go to school or to church . . . or obey anybody; he could go fishing or swimming when and where he chose, and stay as long as it suited him; nobody forbade him to fight; he could sit up as late as he pleased; he was always the first boy that went barefoot in the spring and the last to resume leather in the fall; he never had to wash, nor put on clean clothes . . . In a word, everything that goes to make life precious that boy had."

When the locust trees showered fragrance over the town, Sam would vault over the back fence "me-owing" for Tom Blankenship, and in no time at all Will Bowen, John Briggs, and perhaps one or two others would be climbing Holliday's Hill for a Saturday morning of fun.

Sometimes they would strip to their shirts, blow forest notes on a tin horn, and have at each other with their lath swords, thrusting and parrying in a manner that would have pleased Robin Hood himself. Sometimes they rolled boulders down the hill, and at other times dug for treasure, hour after hour, until they were tired and hot and in need of a cool swim.

Their most exciting game was playing Pirate. They could imagine themselves the owners of a "long, low, black-hulled racer, the *Spirit of the Storm*," with a flag showing the skull and cross-bones of the buccaneer. It was easy to picture them-selves in black velvet doublets and trunks, great jack boots, crimson sashes, belts bristling with horse pistols and blood-stained cutlasses. With a black patch over one eye, several handsome scars, and a brown and weather-beaten look—each pirate now felt himself a match for any ten men on sea or on shore. And rich! The ship was simply loaded with loot. In fact they would never have to dig for treasure again.

High on Holliday's Hill, with the wide Mississippi shimmering below them, and the far blue hills of Illinois in the eastern distance, they had no need of real gold or a real ship, for they already possessed the greatest treasures of this earth—youth and imagination.

If Sam and his gang ever had found gold they would have hidden it in the magnificent cave which nature had furnished for just such a purpose. The cave, in Sam's youth, was owned by an eccentric physician named E. D. McDowell, who operated a medical school in St. Louis. Its labyrinthine windings began some two miles south of Hannibal and a bit back from the river. No one had ever explored its most remote tunnels and caverns. It was believed, however, that these passages wandered for several miles, and perhaps went right under the Mississippi to the Illinois shore. Guns and ammunition had been stored in the cave at times, and it was rumored that gangs of desperadoes had sometimes hidden there. Great flights of bats soared through the winding passages, sometimes extinguishing the flickering candles of the boys and girls who came to the cave each year for a joyous picnic.

In his *Autobiography* Mark Twain says, "I got lost in it myself, along with a lady." Presumably that young lady was Laura Hawkins, and their adventure was the germ of fact around which he wove some of the most exciting pages of *Tom Sawyer.*

You will remember how these two young people wandered from the group of other picnickers in the cave, holding their candles aloft, drifting along and talking happily together as they wound their way "far down into the secret depths of the cave." And you will also remember how they were chased by bats, and stumbled on through the darkness terrified and lost.

"Now, for the first time, the deep stillness of the place laid a clammy hand upon the spirits of the children."

It is never fair to tell the plot of a thrilling story, but no reader has ever been known to put aside *Tom Sawyer* after this boy and girl know they are lost, and begin to realize that they may never again see the sunshine, or the faces of their parents and their friends. How they would have loved to have heard a human voice or to see a friendly candle coming toward them through the utter darkness! The cave was, and is, a fascinating place.

Every bit as exciting is the wooded island in the Mississippi where Sam Clemens, "The Black Avenger of the Spanish Main," Tom Blankenship the "Red-Handed," and John Briggs "The Terror of the Seas" set up their pirate camp, and remained in hiding so long that their desperate families thought all three boys had been drowned.

Nothing has changed on the island—save perhaps a few contours altered by high water. It is still shaded by large trees; and along the sandy paths one may see the delicate footprints of raccoon and fox, rabbit and bird. Cardinals call "what cheer, what cheer." Belted kingfishers dive into the brown waters. There is still a sandbar where boys swim at the head of the island, and good places all along its shore for fishing catfish and white perch. High above the Mississippi a hawk wheels in lazy circles, and far away across the river, Hannibal lies peacefully slumbering. Sometimes the sound of a church bell comes distantly from that town, if it be a Sunday morning, and perhaps one of the last of the sternwheelers will chug by. In a world where no dream seems safe from the despoiler, this island remains as it was when Sam and his friends built their campfire "against the side of a great log twenty or thirty steps within the somber depths of the forest"—pledged eternal loyalty, and began their never-to-be-forgotten adventures.

"After dinner all the gang turned out to hunt for turtle eggs on the bar. They went about poking sticks into the sand, and when they found a soft place they went down on their knees and dug with their hands. Sometimes they would take fifty or sixty eggs out of one hole. They were perfectly round white things a trifle smaller than an English walnut. They had a famous fried egg feast that night, and another on Friday morning.

"After breakfast they went whooping and prancing out on the bar, and chased each other round and round, shedding clothes as they went until they were naked, and then continued the frolic far away up the shoal water of the bar, against the stiff current, which later tripped their legs from under them from time to time and greatly increased the fun."

On they went with their games, splashing water,

blowing, spluttering and laughing until they were exhausted and would sprawl on the dry, hot sand and cover themselves with it and dream and drowse.

Let us leave them there forever, young and brown and happy—on their magic island in the Mississippi —fishing and swimming and perfectly carefree— hoping they will never have to wear clothes again, or face the stern demands of the adult world.

You may well ask what happened to some of the originals of this crew of freebooters. To the great surprise of their teachers, parents, and friends they all grew up to be solid citizens. Albert Bigelow Paine, Mark Twain's first biographer, went to Hannibal to trace the lives of these boys and discovered that three of the Bowen boys became Mississippi River pilots. Will Pitts and John Garth became bankers. John Briggs in time owned a very profitable farm. And even Tom Blankenship—that happy-go-lucky, dirty and lovable boy known to the world as Huckleberry Finn—moved to a western town where he became a respected Justice of the Peace. And we shall see, as this book progresses, what lay in store for Samuel Langhorne Clemens.

As long as they lived, they would all remember

the Hill, the Cave, the Island—and how it felt in those far off and wonderful days to be a boy on the river.

All idyls must end sometime, and Sam Clemens' boyhood ended quite abruptly when he was eleven years and four months old.

John Marshall Clemens' financial problems had increased rather than diminished as the years wore on. He tried to sell the Tennessee land for twenty cents an acre, but no one would buy it. Bravely and desperately he continued his ill-paid work as Justice of the Peace. His dignified face became ever more severe, and his proud eyes more haunted as he watched Jane scrape along by feeding boarders at the family table, and his beloved Pamela travel as much as thirty-five miles to give piano and guitar lessons to eke out the family budget. There was never a hint of a smile now for his redheaded eleven-year-old who was only beginning to sense the family crisis.

The hand of fate moved swiftly in late March of 1847. John Clemens had been seeking the office of

Clerk of the Surrogate Court, a position which would have allowed him to live with dignity if not with ease. So universal was his reputation for honesty and for knowledge of the law that both the Whigs and their rivals the Democrats were willing to vote for him. But John Clemens was taking no chances. A lawsuit in which he was involved was pending at the county seat, and he saw an opportunity to do additional campaigning while in that town. He returned on horseback through a freezing rain, was stricken by pneumonia, and within a few days was obviously dying. When it was apparent to the whole family that he could not live more than a few hours, they gathered at his bedside. From the whole group he called only Pamela to him and kissed her, and then he died.

Sam Clemens was filled with horrible remorse. Why had he given his father and mother so much trouble? The whole world was suddenly bleak and threatening. He ran to his mother and hugged her impulsively and promised that he would follow her every desire from this day on. He would willingly go to work, anything she wished, if she would only allow him to drop out of school. Jane, in her despair, said she was willing. The perpetual summer of boyhood had come to its conclusion as the grim, poverty-stricken family gathered at the grave in the dreary little cemetery north of Hannibal. Ashes to ashes—dust to dust! Slowly the coffin was lowered. John Clemens was at peace at last.

3

NINE YEARS OF TYPESETTING (1848–1857)

To have boyhood vanish overnight, and to have the cares of maturity thrust upon one's shoulders before the age of twelve, seems a cruel burden for a boy who loved his freedom as deeply as did Sam Clemens. But he had made a promise to his mother, and he intended to keep it.

The Clemens family was completely unprepared for their great misfortune. They had no resources of any kind except the seemingly worthless Tennessee land and the little house on Hill Street. At the time Judge Clemens died, Henry was nearly nine, Sam eleven, Pamela nineteen, and Orion—who now became the head of the family—twenty-one. Their only income consisted of the three dollars that Orion sent each week from the wages he received in St. Louis, and the few small coins Pamela could earn teaching the guitar and the piano. In addition there usually was a paying guest at the family table. Even in the "shabby little town" of Hannibal few families were poorer.

Sam Clemens was proud not to add to the burden. At first he took odd jobs, such as clerking briefly in a store. At the age of twelve, probably in October 1848, he followed what was becoming the family pattern. Like Orion before him, and Henry after, he became a printer's devil—that is an unpaid apprentice learning how to hand-set type. He had many other duties too—sweeping up the shop, throwing the broken type in the hellbox, delivering papers, in short anything and everything that needed to be done around a small-town newspaper office.

The master of this apprentice was Joseph P. Ament, who had recently moved his printing business to Hannibal from the nearby town of Palmyra. Ament edited and published a weekly called the *Missouri Courier*—and it was in that obscure little journal that an unsigned line or two of Sam's may first have appeared. Young Clemens was not a reporter, nor a subeditor for the paper—he was the lowest form of life in any print shop, the ink-smeared, grease-smeared boy-of-all-work. But during his two years with Ament he learned to set type swiftly and accurately. As Abraham Lincoln once said, print shops are "the poor man's college."

It is, in fact, virtually impossible to remain completely uneducated while hand-setting column after column of local news and gossip, state news and national news; essays written by schoolteachers and their brighter pupils; poetry copied from classic sources or painfully composed by local versifiers. Often whole novels were run serially, and Sam at his type case read these books the hard way—setting every word in type, then reading the galley proofs against the original to be certain he had made no errors. His excellent spelling was a great help to him in turning out clean proofs; and, although he did not know it, he was learning, by example, how to write.

Life, however, was no bed of roses at the *Missouri Courier*. As Sam would later tell the story: "Mr. Ament, the editor and proprietor of the paper, allowed me the usual emolument of the office of apprentice—that is to say, board and clothes, but no money."

By agreement, Sam was supposed to be supplied with two new suits a year. What he was given instead were hand-me-downs from Ament's wardrobe. Sam was about half as big as his employer and had to turn the cuffs of the pants almost up to his ears to make them short enough. The secondhand shirts gave him the sensation of "living in a circus tent."

Another apprentice in this shop was Wales McCormick, seventeen or eighteen years old, and huge in size. When he dressed in his share of Ament's old clothes, he needed only to flex his muscles or bend over slightly to split the seams. Both boys had a lively sense of humor and made the most of these ill-fitting garments, although they disliked being seen on the streets of Hannibal in cast-off clothing better suited to Tom Blankenship.

Lack of raiment might be tolerated, but lack of food was a far more serious matter for these growing boys. And since clothes and food were all that they received for their labor, they distinctly resented the menu they were served in the slave quarters in the basement of the Ament home. Delicious and savory dishes were carried upstairs to the family table, but none of this good food was ever placed before the ragged apprentices. They were so constantly famished that several times a week they would "hook" potatoes and onions from the Ament cellar. These they transported stealthily to the printing office. Wales had "a secret of cooking a potato which was noble and wonderful and all his own." He was a "reckless, hilarious, admirable creature . . . delightful company." Although often cold and hungry, Sam remembers that while eating their stolen onions and potatoes, and laughing at the penurious Aments and the whole world, they often had "very good times." Still chuckling over the evening's adventure, they would stretch out on their hard pallets on the print shop's grimy floor—their only bed, but good enough for any apprentice according to Ament and his hardhearted wife.

Heartless though he was in many matters, Ament was honorable on one score. Once he had assigned the day's work, he did not ask his apprentices to continue into the evening with added duties. Sometimes, by starting before dawn, Sam could finish his typesetting by the middle of the afternoon. Then he was free to join his old friends and organize an excursion to the island or the cave. Occasionally he went with Laura Hawkins to pick flowers on Holliday's Hill or Lover's Leap. These childhood sweethearts saw each other less frequently as they grew older. Each would eventually marry another; but they would remain tender friends throughout life.

Sometimes when he had earned a few hours of

freedom Sam would spend it with his mother and Pamela and Henry—all of whom he loved dearly. Jane Clemens was standing up well in her widowhood—a little quieter now and more likely in her few spare moments to turn to her exquisite embroidery than to click her heels to the rhythm of Pamela's guitar. Pamela, serious minded, shy and in delicate health, appeared to be destined to the role of lifelong companion to her mother.

Young Henry's fair and curly head was simply crammed with information. He was the most avid reader in the family; sweet-tempered, thoughtful and merry—a great comfort to them all.

But it was Sam who worried his mother the most —as he always had. Not because he was mischievous, for very seldom now did he play high-spirited pranks after his long day's work; but rather because his young face in repose sometimes showed a swift shadow of melancholy. She was proud of this boy laboring so diligently, and keeping his hard promise.

The late Judge Clemens had included among his many dreams the vision of a newspaper, owned and operated by the family, and published in Hannibal.

His widow now remembered that dream, and, hoping to hold her brood together, began writing letters to Orion in St. Louis. If Orion would come home and start a newspaper, Sam would become his journeyman printer and Henry his apprentice. It might have worked under any management except that of the goodhearted but utterly impractical Orion Clemens.

Orion was a saintly person, completely meek and utterly honest. He was a handsome young man, with some of Jane's warmth and all of his father's capacity for failure. He had wanted to be a lawyer and a political orator. But the long, hard road to such eminence had proved far beyond his native ability and his patience.

Orion had the constancy of a butterfly. Each morning he awoke with some burning enthusiasm— a new way to make himself rich and famous. By evening the fire was usually out, and he was in the depths of despair. As the family well knew, Orion changed his religion and his politics almost as often as he changed his shirts. But one thing he never altered was his tolerance for all men, even those who were his enemies. Jane was sometimes exasperated with this son of hers who continually "turned the other cheek."

However, Orion was an excellent printer, and his mother believed that if he started a newspaper in Hannibal it might well succeed. She was immeasurably happy when in 1850 he left his well-paid job in St. Louis and arrived on the upriver packet filled with hope for the new adventure.

According to plan, Henry now became an apprentice; and Sam was easily lured from Ament's *Courier* with the princely promise of three and one half dollars a week. Orion was never able to pay Sam a single cent in wages, but at least the three Clemens brothers had the exciting experience of running their own paper—a feeble little weekly called *Western Union*. Some ten months later, in 1851, Orion made three fatal mistakes: he bought out a rival paper for $500—the money borrowed from a local farmer at ten per cent interest; he lowered the advertising rate, and he lowered the subscription rate. The combined papers, published as the *Hannibal Journal*, never had a chance.

For Sam, however, it was a step up in the world. Theoretically, at least, he was now working for wages. On a more substantial level, he now slept in a real bed—his old one in the back bedroom of the house on Hill Street. And the family meals were his mother's own cooking. Food, presumably, was not a problem since the one-dollar-a-year subscription to the *Journal* was usually paid in eggs, poultry, meat, fruit, vegetables, cordwood—or almost anything else except coin of the realm. Unfortunately Orion could not use crocks of butter or a few bushels of potatoes to buy paper, ink, type metal, and parts for his ancient printing machinery. For these supplies he needed something he never possessed—cash money! They survived, these days, on family loyalty—on Orion's dreams, Sam's wit, Henry's bright charm, Pamela's music, and Jane Clemens' love and courage.

In September 1851 some of the music went out of their lives. Pamela, who had just turned twenty-four, and who was in serious danger of becoming an old maid, received and accepted her first proposal. Will Moffett was no prince charming, but he was a serious and solid citizen, a long-time friend of the family, who had become a prosperous commission merchant in St. Louis. Everyone in the Clemens household wished the couple well as they left for the traditional trip to Niagara Falls. Jane, more than any of the others, missed the company of Pamela, and the soft throbbing of the guitar. She had lost three children and her husband by death—and her only living daughter, by marriage. More than ever she now awaited the return each evening of her three weary, ink-stained young men, making it a point to be cheerful for their sakes, as they were cheerful for hers, although the business was failing miserably.

If Orion had followed the suggestions of his brother Sam, the paper might well have prospered. Sam thought the *Journal* was dull, stuffy, and boring—too flat, stale, and pompous ever to awaken the sleepy town of Hannibal. Sam's idea was to fill the weekly with verbal firecrackers that would jolt the readers out of their beds, stir up controversy, and start the village chattering like a tree full of magpies. Sam's style of writing was still crude in the extreme, but sprinkled with cayenne pepper and gunpowder. Essentially young Clemens was a gentle person— affectionate and loyal to family and comrades. But he was also a clown, a showman, and a mischief-maker who delighted in deflating stuffed shirts. Whenever Orion left town, Sam became editor of the paper. Immediately he took full advantage of the

opportunity, filling the columns with slashing humor, bad puns, and silly but biting satire—often
aimed at the opposition press. One rival editor, poor
fellow, was driven from town by his young tormen-
tor, who pictured him in a rough drawing testing the
depth of the water as he cautiously entered the
river's edge where, it was rumored, he had threatened to commit suicide.

Most of Sam's humor, however, was not mali-
cious, but merely playful and high spirited. He wrote
what he considered howlingly funny parodies on the
sentimental poetry of the era. And often for filler he
would insert some such line as:

> An old lady in Jersey
> (To be continued.)

At least once during this interim he managed to
place a short sketch with an allegedly humorous pe-
riodical called *The Carpet-Bag,* which was edited in
Boston. This first magazine piece by the upcoming
author is entitled "The Dandy Frightening the
Squatter." It tells of an overdressed eastern dude
with a "killing moustache" who steps from a steamboat at Hannibal to threaten a local squatter with
two pistols and a Bowie knife. The frontiersman

calmly tosses the dandy into the river, picks up the pistols and the knife and walks away, with a devastating taunt to the wet and crest-fallen easterner.

The anecdote is no better and no worse than most of the other frontier humor of the day, although it seems ironical that it should have been published in the relatively sedate and cultured Boston of Emerson, Longfellow, Thoreau, and James Russell Lowell.

Sam's opportunities to enliven the *Hannibal Journal* were few and far between. Orion kept him at the type case longer hours each day than even Ament had, and distinctly frowned upon his mischievous editing when he was temporarily away from town. Slowly the paper suffocated in reams of deadly trivia, while a young redheaded typesetter grew increasingly restless with his pointless and unpaid labor.

To ease the monotony, Sam attended every form of traveling amusement that came to town, minstrel shows, lectures, showboat entertainments, and the demonstrations given by mesmerizers and phrenologists. Using the free tickets always supplied to newspapers, Sam could even escort a girl to these performances. Somewhere he had acquired a handsome coat with a bright plaid lining, which he wore with dash and bravado. He could also play both the guitar and the piano—in a rather primitive manner; thus he could serenade the young ladies, strumming the chords to accompany his fine tenor voice. Life was not utterly dreary during his teens—in fact, being the person he was, life would always have vitality for Samuel Langhorne Clemens; his self-generating spark machine never ran out of electricity.

At about this time an odd little happenstance made a deep impression on Sam's mind. One day, as he was walking along the street, a page torn from a book fluttered across his path. He picked it up, and was immediately fascinated as he read of Joan of Arc— the Maid of Orleans in shining armor—leading her troops against the invading English. Even Robin Hood was a dull figure compared to this teen-age girl who helped to crown the dauphin, and finally died at the stake. Immediately the young printer ransacked the local bookstore and the library (of which Orion was now president) seeking more information about Joan of Arc. From Joan, he proceeded to French history, American history, and World history.

Never an avid reader until this time, Sam now began to devour every book he could find. It must have amazed his recent teachers to discover him browsing at the bookstore. Joan of Arc was a romantic personality with a great cause. It added to Sam's restlessness to realize that he, Sam Clemens, seemed doomed to live out a dreary life in a drowsy town. No shining armor for him, unless he soon made a break for freedom.

It had been obvious from the first that Orion's paper would fail. Moreover, the gentle Orion in his desperation, was now—to use his own words—practicing "tyranny" toward his overworked journeyman printer. During the final days of the collapsing enterprise in 1853, when Sam was nearly eighteen years of age, he decided to seek his fortune elsewhere. His mother, realizing the inevitable, consented. She asked him to place his hand upon the Bible and to swear that while he was away he would not touch a drop of liquor or "throw a card." Sam promised and he kept his promise.

Clemens himself briefly summarizes the next stage of his life in his *Autobiography*:

"I disappeared one night and fled to St. Louis. There I worked in the composing-room of the

Evening News for a time and then started on my travels to see the world. The world was New York City and there was a little World's Fair there. It had just been opened . . . I arrived in New York with two or three dollars in pocket change and a ten-dollar bank bill concealed in the lining of my coat. I got work at villainous wages . . . and I found board in a sufficiently villainous mechanics' boarding-house in Duane Street . . . By and by I went to Philadelphia and worked there some months as a 'sub' on the *Inquirer* and the *Public Ledger.* Finally I made a flying trip to Washington to see the sights there, and in 1854 I went back to the Mississippi Valley, sitting upright in the smoking-car two or three days and nights. When I reached St. Louis I was exhausted. I went to bed on board a steamboat that was bound [upriver] for Muscatine. I fell asleep at once, with my clothes on, and didn't wake again for thirty-six hours."

Orion had transferred his unprofitable printing business to Keokuk, Iowa. Sam, who had intended only a brief visit, could not resist his brother's plea to remain and help him. The results were a weary repetition of the past—months of hard work with no wages. The drab years dragged on and on. Sam knew that somehow he must make a bold stroke to save his whole family from poverty.

At about this time he ran across a glowing report made by U.S. Navy Lieutenant William Lewis Herndon, who was the first North American to float the length of the great Amazon River. Rivers would always intrigue Sam Clemens, and here was a mighty stream, larger and more romantic than even his beloved Mississippi. He wanted to see the Indians with their blow guns, screaming monkeys racing through the treetops, and parrots and other jungle birds in their rainbow colors. Besides, here was evidence that an intrepid adventurer might win a fortune growing and marketing cocoa.

The first leg of this proposed journey took him to Cincinnati, where he spent several months setting type, saving almost every cent of his wages to help finance the trip. Still dreaming of the Amazon, he watched the late snows melt, and the first buds appear.

4

PILOT ON THE MISSISSIPPI (1857–1861)

It was spring in Cincinnati—April of the year 1857. The willows were wearing their new green, and the forest floor was freshly garnished with small blossoms pushing their way through the brown carpet of last year's leaves. Up the vast Mississippi Valley, up the Ohio and into the open window of Sam's bedroom came the surge of the new season, a restless time for all humanity, but particularly for a young man of twenty-one. Sam saw, up the river, a little side-wheeler edging toward the Ohio shore to make a landing.

His rent was paid and his carpetbags were packed. Safe in his pocket was the precious ticket paying his fare to New Orleans. Who could tell? By this time next year he might be far up the steaming Amazon, well on his way toward making his fortune in cocoa. Snatching up his bags, Sam started for the dock, feeling as cheerful as the choir of birds that sang from every garden.

Once aboard the venerable *Paul Jones,* Sam's old love of the river swiftly reasserted itself. With deep satisfaction he felt the pulse of the engines, heard the hiss of steam and the churning of the great paddle wheels slap-slapping the waters of the placid Ohio. Blue shores drifted slowly sternward as the lazy river boat, aided by the current, began its long journey.

Sam soon made the acquaintance of the story-telling night watchman, and of the bearded, burly, and hard-swearing mate. But the boat was many miles down the river before he had the courage to enter the sacred and forbidden pilot house where Horace Bixby stood at the wheel, nonchalant and self-assured. The pilot of the *Paul Jones* was cool and silent for a time, completely ignoring this young interloper with the engaging grin and amusing drawl. It was "Sammy's long-talk" that finally intrigued him into asking where he had ever learned such an odd way of speaking. Sam referred the pilot to his mother, saying that she talked that way too. Bixby took his eyes from the river, and for several moments surveyed his uninvited visitor. What he saw seemed to please him—steady blue-green eyes with a glint of merriment, a friendly and slightly impertinent face, unruly auburn curls, and a pervading air of lively intelligence that no drawl in the world could completely hide.

Long before they reached New Orleans, Horace Bixby was letting Sam take the wheel, but only on the broad, deep, safe stretches of the river where Bixby feared neither snag nor shoal. Sam wished his old friends in Hannibal could see him now, guiding the *Paul Jones* as cleverly as any real pilot. But Bixby was sitting conveniently nearby on the pilot's bench, watching Sam like a hawk, judging his character too as they eased southward into the land of slavery, sugar and cotton.

In New Orleans Sam found to his dismay that there was no ship scheduled for a voyage to Para, Brazil (at the mouth of the Amazon). In fact there might not be another boat for "ten or twelve years." Sam was momentarily deeply depressed. There went another of his dreams like a bursting soap bubble! Then a happy alternative occurred to him. He remembered that "permanent ambition" of every boy in Hannibal to be a river pilot, and he raced to the dock where the *Paul Jones* was unloading. He pleaded with Horace Bixby to be allowed to become a "cub" under Bixby's tutelage.

Bixby used every argument he could devise to dissuade him. He pointed out to Sam that a cub had to work for at least eighteen months for nothing but food and sleeping quarters, and even so might never become sufficiently expert to be granted a pilot's license. He told this eager young applicant that learning the river was the most difficult feat that had ever tormented the human brain; that memorizing all the stars in the sky was easier. And he finally pointed out that cubs ordinarily paid a stiff fee, at least $500, to the pilot who took on the task of teaching them the river.

Sam said he would gladly pay the $500, one fifth down, and the rest from his wages when he became a licensed pilot.

Bixby sighed, and consented.

On the first afternoon, when they backed out of the great line of steamships tied up at New Orleans and started on the upriver run to St. Louis, Bixby immediately gave Sam the wheel and told him to "shave those steamships as close as you'd peel an apple." Sam, thinking this was a crazy order, gave the other boats a much wider berth. Bixby exploded, took the wheel himself, and with the greatest ease "trimmed the ships so closely that disaster seemed ceaselessly imminent." Bixby was not being foolhardy, as Sam was later to learn. A pilot had to be able to handle his quarter-of-a-million-dollar boat, with its precious cargo of humanity and freight, as precisely as though he were doing figure skating on an ice rink. In a crisis, such delicacy and good judgment were all that could save the ship.

To understand fully the almost incredible difficulties of learning the river in the era before there were marked channels, buoys and lights, the reader must turn to Mark Twain's *Life on the Mississippi*—a delightful account of his years as a pilot. In those days the only accurate map of those hundreds of winding miles of treacherous water was in the mind of the pilot himself.

For instance, in the 1,200 miles between New Orleans and St. Louis there were more than 500 dangerous shoals, one of which had destroyed more than twenty steamboats. The pilot not only needed to understand how to avoid or "climb over" such shallows, but must also know like the palm of his hand every reef, bar, towhead, and island; every point, crossing, and chute. Snags that could rip the bottom out of a boat were constantly changing position. Channels were continuously shifting.

On his first trip upstream, Sam Clemens discovered an added difficulty. Pilots worked "four hours on, and four hours off." And so, although Sam filled notebooks with the lore that Bixby taught him as they stood together in the pilot house, there were four-hour gaps in his information while he rested or slept—gaps that must be filled on subsequent trips. To complicate things still further, Sam found that in coming down the river, everything had to be learned all over again and in reverse, since no landmark, point, island, or reef had the same appearance as it did going up. In addition, all distances were altered by darkness.

"My boy," said Bixby, "you've got to know the *shape* of the river perfectly. It is all there is left to steer by on a very dark night. Everything else is blotted out and gone. But mind you, it hasn't the same shape in the night that it has in the daytime."

"How on earth am I ever going to learn it, then?"

"How do you follow a hall at home in the dark? Because you know the shape of it. You can't see it."

"Do you mean to say that I've got to know all the million trifling variations of shape in the banks of this interminable river as well as I know the shape of the front hall at home?"

"On my honor you've got to know them *better* than any man ever did know the shapes of the halls in his own house."

"I wish I was dead!"

Bixby had not exaggerated when he had warned Sam that learning the Mississippi was no simple task. The river seldom looked the same on any two nights or in any two phases of the moon. Clear starlight threw one kind of shadow, a pitch-black night another, and a night of gray mist was a different and even greater problem. The burning piles of sugarcane waste on the lower river reduced visibility to absolute zero at night and dimmed and distorted the atmosphere with whirling, drifting smoke even on otherwise bright days.

Sam was just beginning to adjust his addled brain to all these variations when a new complex of problems appeared. The early summer rise in the river changed all the points, landmarks, and islands again, creating chutes through oxbows which both lured and endangered the river boats. Most of these chutes that cut across wide bends were so narrow that a ship could not turn around, once it had made the decision to run the chute. At the head of the chute there was often dangerously shallow water where a steamboat could go aground and sit for hours, days, or weeks awaiting higher water. To anticipate such danger, the leadsmen constantly tested the depth of the channel, crying a familiar chant: "Mark three! Quarter twain! Mark twain, mark twain, mark twain!" *Mark twain* meant two fathoms of water, or a safe twelve feet. It was always a welcome cry.

While still a cub, Sam purchased a smart blue coat, white trousers, and patent leather shoes, and these he wore with a jaunty air in the gleaming pilot houses of many a river boat. It was pleasant to be awarded a respectful "Sir" by the waiters, the barber, and almost everyone else aboard these handsome ships. And he particularly fancied the figure he cut with the gay groups gathered around the piano while he played and sang:

An old, old horse whose name was
Methusalem,
Took him down and sold him in Jerusalem,
A long time ago.

Those were gaudy days on the river. The big boats were infested with gamblers and other shady riffraff. But Sam continued to remember his promise to his mother. He did not gamble nor drink during his river years. But he did keep his eyes wide open. Long afterward he was to say that he never encountered a character in life or in fiction that he had not previously met on the river. Wealthy planters and their wives; Black roustabouts and singers; hopeful settlers and their families—in fact a wide cross section of the restless nation—fighting, courting, dreaming of riches; arguing politics and religion! Mankind on the move! What magnificent material for this yarn-spinning cub pilot who would one day become a writer!

In New Orleans he liked to roam the streets watching crowds of a dozen tints, laughing, dancing, walking sedately toward the cathedral. At the St. Louis end of his run he had the even richer emotional experience of spending his time with his lively family. Will and Pamela Moffett had purchased a larger home so that Jane Clemens could live with them many months of each year. This big house also provided Orion, Henry, and Sam with comfortable quarters when they came to visit. No wonder Sam Clemens would always look back upon this period with nostalgia. But a dark event, looming like a fog over the river, would soon dim these months of sunshine.

One night, while sleeping at the Moffett house on Locust Street in St. Louis, Sam had a dream so vivid that he thought it was real. In the dream he saw his brother Henry lying dead in a metal casket. Henry was wearing a suit of Sam's clothing, and on his breast was a large bouquet of white roses, with one red rose at its center. Sam could not shake the dream from his mind for half an hour after waking, and was only convinced that it *was* a dream when he saw his younger brother alive and eating a hearty breakfast.

Both boys were now working on a much-admired boat called the *Pennsylvania*—Sam as an unpaid cub pilot and Henry as an equally unpaid "mud" clerk. Because he had wanted Henry near him, and because he was certain his brother would rise in due time to well-paid clerkships and eventually "purser" of the boat, Sam had used his influence to get him the job. It was now time to go aboard for the down-river trip, and in the usual manner of the Clemens family, everyone shook hands upon departure.

But when Henry had reached the street, Jane Clemens did a strange thing; she called this youngest son back to the door, and shook his hand a second time, holding it longer and more tenderly than was her custom. Sam Clemens took note of this and was again disturbed. The brothers were unusually silent as they walked to the dock.

In one respect, Henry's job was preferable to Sam's on that "swift and popular" packet. Bixby had lent Sam to Tom Brown, the expert but tyrannical pilot of the *Pennsylvania*, whose method of teaching a young wheelsman was to humiliate him on every possible occasion. Henry did not work directly under the pilot. His supreme commander was Captain Kleinfelter, a fatherly man who was always considerate toward both Sam and Henry.

Pilot Brown was a coarse, illiterate, and brutal dictator, feared by every cub on the river. He had given Sam Clemens some of the most miserable weeks of his life, constantly devising new ways to upbraid and crush him. Nothing Sam did for Brown was ever satisfactory. If he sheared away from a dangerous reef, Sam was a "yellow coward," but if he took the reef closely, Brown roared "you numbskull, you derned mud cat!"

On this trip downstream, an incident occurred which Sam would always remember. Captain Kleinfelter sent Henry to tell Pilot Brown that he wanted him to stop at a certain plantation to pick up freight. Henry dutifully complied. But the pilot gave no intimation that he had heard the request or intended to stop. That was his usual imperious manner of treating underclerks. Sam sized up the situation and sensed trouble brewing. Tom Brown was deaf, but would not admit it, and if he sailed by the plantation (as presently he did) poor Henry might get the blame.

As the *Pennsylvania* steamed serenely past the appointed stop, Captain Kleinfelter appeared in the pilot house and said to Brown: "Let her come around, sir, let her come around! Didn't Henry tell you to land here?"

"*No*, sir!"

"I sent him up to do it."

"He *did* come up; and that's all the good it done, the dod-derned fool. He never said anything."

Sam didn't want to become embroiled in this argument, but when the captain asked him whether he had heard Henry give his message, Sam bravely answered: "Yes, sir!"

Brown was furious and promised that he would teach both boys a lesson they would not soon forget. An hour later when Henry entered the pilot house, all unsuspecting of any trouble, Brown turned upon him, his face blazing with anger: "Here! Why didn't you tell me we'd got to land at that plantation?"

"I did tell you, Mr. Brown."

"It's a lie!"

"You lie yourself. He did tell you," Sam Clemens said.

Brown glared at Sam, then started menacingly toward Henry. Sam knew he could be put in prison for mutiny against his chief. But while he was willing to take abuse himself, he was not prepared to let this tyrant threaten or attack his younger brother. As Henry turned to leave, Brown snatched from a hod beside the stove "a ten pound lump of coal" and sprang after Henry. Sam grabbed a heavy stool and intercepted him with a blow so well calculated that it laid the bully on the floor. Then Sam got astride the pilot and began pummeling him with his fists.

For his act of insubordination he was sure he would go to a federal prison. But first he was going to give Brown his well-deserved beating.

Very shortly thereafter Sam was called into Captain Kleinfelter's cabin at the other end of the Texas deck for what he felt certain would be dismissal, disgrace or worse.

"So you've been fighting Mr. Brown?" the captain asked.

"Yes, sir."

"Do you know that that is a very serious matter?"

"Yes, sir."

"Are you aware that this boat was plowing down the river fully five minutes with no one at the wheel?"

"Yes, sir."

"Did you strike him first?"

"Yes, sir."

"What with?"

"A stool, sir."

"Hard?"

"Middling, sir."

"Did it knock him down?"

"He—he fell, sir."

"Did you follow it up? Did you do anything further?"

"Yes, sir."

"What did you do?"

"Pounded him, sir."

"Pounded him?"

"Yes, sir."

"Did you pound him much? That is, severely?"

"One might call it that, sir, maybe."

"I'm deuced glad of it! Hark ye, never mention that I said that. You have been guilty of a great crime; and don't you ever be guilty of it again, on this boat. *But*—lay for him ashore. Give him a good sound thrashing, do you hear? I'll pay the expenses. Now go—and mind you, not a word of this to anybody. Clear out with you! You've been guilty of a great crime, you whelp."

When the boat reached New Orleans Sam did not attempt to give Brown a second thrashing. But Brown himself brought matters to a climax by informing Captain Kleinfelter that he would no longer pilot a boat on which Sam Clemens was a wheelsman. Kleinfelter instantly accepted Brown's resignation and offered Sam—still an unlicensed pilot—the glamorous opportunity of being the full-fledged pilot of the *Pennsylvania* on its return trip to St. Louis. Sam was deeply grateful for this vote of confidence. But he was also aware that he had served only one year of his apprenticeship and was not yet ready for the assignment. Kleinfelter searched the port for a new pilot, but without success. With disgust he rehired Brown, procuring for Sam a passage on a later ship, the *A. T. Lacey*. New arrangements would be made at the St. Louis terminus, and Sam would again be wheelsman of the *Pennsylvania*.

It took a boat several days to make a turn-around —unloading freight and loading a new cargo. During these periods in New Orleans Sam often took a night watchman's job guarding the freight piles on the levee, thus earning the only spending money available. Henry joined him one night and they talked from sunset to sunrise about the family; about the fight with Brown; about the old days in Hannibal. Sam, who always loved the midnight sky, pointed out the various constellations in the velvet darkness above them. Then, for reasons he would never fathom, Sam began giving Henry manly, but fatal advice. He said:

"In case of disaster to the boat, don't lose your head—leave that unwisdom to the passengers—they are competent—they'll attend to it. But you rush for the hurricane deck, and astern of the solitary lifeboat lashed aft the wheelhouse on the port side, and obey the mate's orders—thus you will be useful. When the boat is launched, give such help as you can in getting the women and children into it, and be sure you don't try to get into it yourself. It is summer weather, the river is only a mile wide as a rule, and you can swim ashore without trouble."

The *Pennsylvania* started upriver before the *A. T. Lacey.* Just below Memphis its boilers exploded, demolishing most of the ship and killing more than 150 people including Pilot Brown. Henry Clemens was blown through the air fifty feet from the boat, but believing himself not badly hurt came swimming back to the burning vessel to follow Sam's advice—helping the women, the children, and the wounded. Henry, however, had been injured far more seriously than he realized. He had breathed live steam and had been terribly scalded.

Sam, in an agony of anxiety, reached Memphis about two days after the accident. He found Henry lying with some forty other seriously injured passengers and crewmen in a public building, where Memphis physicians and volunteer ladies of mercy were doing all that was humanly possible to save their lives. For six days and nights, almost without sleep, Sam hovered at Henry's side; and on the last day a kindly physician offered a ray of hope. But during the night an incompetent intern administered an overdose of morphine, and the next morning Henry was dead. Sam, out of exhaustion, and believing his brother safe, had fallen into a fitful sleep.

Upon awakening he was terrified to find Henry gone. He hurried to the adjoining room serving as a morgue. And there he saw his dream in every detail come true. There lay Henry, pale and dead in a metal casket. He was wearing a suit of Sam's clothing taken from his luggage. And at just this moment the ladies of mercy entered the room with a large bouquet of white roses, with one red rose at the center. This they laid tenderly on the breast of a boy who had never done anyone in the world the slightest harm—the good, bright, cheerful youngest son of Jane Clemens.

Sam said that his hair turned gray overnight. And if that is a slight exaggeration, the fact remains that the loss of Henry hurt him more deeply than the loss of any brother or sister.

Soon Sam had secured his license as a pilot, and he apparently enjoyed his brief years in that capacity on the river. But it is worth noting that throughout his life he wrote very little about the ensuing years when he was master of many a proud vessel plying between New Orleans and St. Louis. His greatest satisfaction, perhaps, was to contribute generously to the welfare of his mother, and his always unsuccessful brother Orion. At least once he had the pleasure of taking Jane Clemens to New Orleans to see the gay sights, to tap her heels to the strange music, and to eat in the exotic restaurants.

The romantic years of river steamboating were drawing to a close—hastened by the angry rumble of voices and drums and cannon. Lincoln was presently taking the oath of office and the South Carolinians had soon fired on Fort Sumter. Now every pilot had to make a swift decision, whether to stay in the South, or leave for the North. Sam helped to pilot the last steamship going upriver, escaping

the blockade "close as you'd peel an apple"—
Memphis, Cairo, and now the steeples and chimneys
of St. Louis. Nervous cannoneers at the Jefferson
Barracks wrote a crashing finale to these river years.
They fired two shots at Sam's ship as it moved into
port—the second one smashing the glass of the pilot
house.

Sam thought the Civil War would be a brief af-
fair, and that, following a few months fighting, peace
would be signed. He could then go back to many
years of piloting. He had no way of knowing that
his river days had ended. They would continue in his
dreams, however, for the remainder of his life, with
the chant of the leadsman ringing forever in his ears:
"Mark twain! Mark twain! Mark twain!"

5

SOLDIER, MINER AND JOURNALIST (1861–1867)

When Sam Clemens returned to St. Louis on his final trip north he was a thoroughly perplexed young man. Like thousands of other Missourians he was not quite sure which side he favored, the Union or the Confederacy. He had been born into a slave-owning family, but his lifelong attitude toward Blacks was one of sympathy and respect. Orion by this time was an abolitionist and a staunch supporter of Abraham Lincoln. Missouri was split through and through with dissension over the slavery issue, with brother suspecting brother and neighbor hating neighbor. Then, to complicate matters still further, the state was "invaded" by Union forces. Governor "Claib" Jackson called for 50,000 volunteer militia to defend the State of Missouri.

Sam, who was visiting in Hannibal at the time,

now saw a reasonable cause, based on local patriot-
ism—and he served that cause faithfully for about
three weeks. Some of the boys he had known since
childhood were forming a little company which they
called the "Marion Rangers" and they asked Sam to
share the fun. It sounded as though it might be a
lark, very much like the old days when his gang had
met in secret to pledge eternal allegiance to the pirate brotherhood and to plan their next raid on
some well-defended peach orchard.

Fifteen of these young men held just such a secret
and nocturnal meeting in the Bear Creek Woods and
elected their officers. Tom Lyman, a young fellow
with "a good deal of spirit" but with "no military
experience," was made captain. Sam was unani-
mously chosen as second lieutenant. In fact so many
officers and noncommissioned officers were elected
that only a few were left to play the humble role of
private. The entire company, privates and officers
alike, would leave their camp entirely exposed to the
enemy while they wandered off to see their best
girls, or to have dinner with friends. It was a very re-
laxed company—without uniforms, flag, or disci-
pline. No one would take orders from anyone else.
Their equipment consisted of a few old blankets and

frying pans, some ancient shotguns, and an abundance of good humor.

Usually the camp was deserted while the brave
soldiers amused themselves elsewhere. But on an
evening convenient to all, they kissed their girls
good-bye and gathered for their first march to a village called New London in Ralls County. It would
have been much too simple and unexciting to walk
down the road. It lacked the air of secrecy, mystery,
and danger. So Tom Lyman took them cross-country
through the dark woods. For the first hour they sang
songs and joked as they stumbled over logs, fell into
ravines, and otherwise enjoyed their outing. During
the second and third hours there was less singing
and more swearing.

At the end of four hours they had completed their
ten-mile trek, and straggled into New London
"soiled, heel-blistered, fagged." They stacked their
shotguns in the barn of Colonel Ralls, an oily-
tongued veteran of the Mexican War, and gladly accepted his invitation to a good Missouri breakfast:
hot biscuits, hot corn pone, fried chicken, bacon,
coffee, eggs, milk, buttermilk—in fact just the fare
to convince the "Marion Rangers" that war has its
pleasant moments.

After the last fried chicken had been demolished, the Colonel led them to a nearby meadow, and there, beneath the shade of a tree, told them what a brave little company they were. Around Sam's waist he strapped a sword that had seen heroic service in the Mexican War. Then Ralls made a resounding speech filled with patriotic fire, spread-eagle oratory, and double-talk. He told his sleepy visitors that they were supposed to fight, and if need be, to die bravely! He made each man place his hand on the Bible and swear that he would be "faithful to the State of Missouri and drive all invaders from her soil, no matter whence they might come or under what flag they might march."

"This mixed us up considerably," Lieutenant Clemens would later admit, "and we could not make out just what service we were embarked in." Since about half the company had vague Union sympathies and the other half vague Confederate ones, they were agreed on only two things: first, that they would be loyal to Missouri; and second, that they were going to spend a few delightful weeks together until the war blew over.

"Then," says Sam, "we formed in line of battle and marched four miles to a shady and pleasant piece of woods, on the border of the far-reaching expanses of a flowery prairie. It was an enchanting region for war—our kind of war. We took up a strong position, with some low, rocky, and wooded hills behind us and a purling, limpid creek in front. Straightway half the command were in swimming and the other half fishing."

This "strong position" was in fact an old maple-sugar camp. It had a well, with a rope and bucket, and a corncrib where the company spread their blankets. Sometimes in the night a rat would creep in to gnaw the corn. A militiaman, in irritation, would throw an ear of corn at the rat, usually hitting a fellow soldier by mistake. In a matter of seconds the entire corncrib would be bedlam, and a battle royal would ensue. "The ears were half as heavy as bricks and when they struck they hurt."

Life was always lively at Camp Ralls (as they called their cantonment). But it became much livelier when nearby farmers began arriving with an assortment of old horses to alter the company, presto, from mere foot soldiers into proud cavalry! Sam's mount was an evil-tempered little mule that bucked him high into the air every time Sam tried to straddle him, and sat down and sulked if anyone tried to lead him. Many of the other chargers were equally co-operative. None of these boys were horsemen, but in time they learned to ride well enough to go serenading the local farm girls.

Sam says that for a time "life was idly delicious, it was perfect; there was nothing to mar it. Then came some farmers with an alarm one day." And this was but the first of many such alarms, for an Illinois regiment under a very businesslike colonel named Ulysses S. Grant was combing the country-side for Missouri militia. Sam had never previously heard of Grant, who in later years would become his friend and his idol. But at this particular time, Grant might have shot young Clemens if he had come upon his little company of Confederates.

Fifteen boys with outmoded guns facing a Union regiment! War each day seemed less like a picnic as these militiamen retreated, retreated, and fled again. Even with the enemy at hand, none of the company would stand sentry duty at night, particularly if it was raining. They huddled together for protection, sure that every cracking twig was the footstep of a Union soldier seeking their camp under cover of darkness.

And that is how an incident occurred which

made war forever horrible to Sam Clemens. Another warning had come of Union cavalry in the neighborhood. That night they heard the sound of a horse's hooves, saw a mounted man and thought they could make out other horsemen following. The moon was behind a cloud, but they could clearly see one figure on horseback silhouetted against the sky. Six of the men, including Sam, fired almost simultaneously.

After the roar of the guns and the first commotion, they could hear nothing. The expected attack did not materialize.

"There was not a sound, not the whisper of a leaf; just perfect stillness, an uncanny kind of stillness, which was all the more uncanny on account of the damp, earthy, late-night smells now rising and pervading it. Then, wondering, we crept stealthily out and approached the man. When we got to him the moon revealed him distinctly."

He was lying on his back, his white shirt splashed with blood, his breath coming painfully. Sam suddenly thought of himself as a murderer. He had helped to kill this unknown man who had done him no injury, a human being cherishing life like any other man.

"That was the coldest sensation that ever went

through my marrow. I was down by him in a moment helplessly stroking his forehead, and I would have given anything then—my own life freely—to make him again what he had been five minutes before. And all the boys seemed to be feeling in the same way; they hung over him full of pitying interest, and tried all they could do to help him and said all sorts of regretful things. They had forgotten all about the enemy, they thought only of this one forlorn unit of the foe . . . He muttered and mumbled like a dreamer in his sleep about his wife and child, and I thought with a new despair, 'This thing I have done does not end with him' . . . And it seemed an epitome of war, that all war must be that, the killing of strangers against whom you feel no personal animosity, strangers whom in other circumstances you would help if you found them in trouble, and who would help you if you needed it. My campaign was spoiled. It seemed to me that I was not rightly equipped for this awful business."

Sam and his friends were as brave as the other participants who fought in the Civil War—braver than many, perhaps, since they could still feel compassion. Some of them would later distinguish themselves on one battlefront or another. But ill equipped, untrained, without a leader—these summer soldiers, filled with romantic, tender feelings for mankind, were not conditioned to the grim business of systematic killing. They had voted themselves into this war, and now they voted themselves out. Sam Clemens, torn by grief over this tragedy, with a badly sprained ankle and running a high fever, did not cast his vote against the disbanding of the "Marion Rangers."

The death of the stranger, however, should not have haunted his memory (as it did, for many years). Sam could scarcely have been responsible for that killing. Throughout his life he proved beyond doubt that he could never hit even the largest target with a gun. Some other marksman among the boys brought down that lonely man on horseback on that summer night, long ago, in Missouri.

Four anguished years of the Civil War were yet ahead. More than half a million young men in blue and gray would leave their bones upon its battlefields. But for Sam Clemens—who still predicted a brief conflict—there would be no further killing of strangers.

In a roundabout way, it was President Lincoln

who kept Sam from any further participation in the war. Lincoln had chosen as his Attorney General a prominent St. Louis lawyer named Edward Bates, a close friend of Orion Clemens. Bates secured for Orion the post of Secretary of Nevada Territory. And Orion asked Sam to come along as the unpaid secretary to the Secretary.

There was an additional convenience in taking Sam. He had a big bag of silver coins saved during his years as a river pilot, and Orion, who was always penniless, needed some of that money for his transportation westward. He was grateful when Sam bought two steamboat tickets to carry them from St. Louis to St. Joseph, where they disembarked. He was grateful again when Sam dug deeply into the sack for an additional $300, their fares on the Overland Stage during the twenty days and nights of travel between St. Joseph, Missouri, and Carson City, Nevada.

At St. Joe they discovered with dismay that they were each allowed only twenty-five pounds of baggage on the coach. Orion insisted upon retaining a six-pound unabridged dictionary. But they discarded with regret their swallow-tail coats, white kid gloves, stovepipe hats and other fancy regalia. These were shipped back to St. Louis.

Two less experienced tenderfeet had seldom invaded the West. Orion had a very small Colt's revolver, which he carried unloaded to prevent accident. Sam was "armed to the teeth with a pitiful little Smith and Wesson's seven-shooter, which carried a ball like a homoeopathic pill." The only other passenger on most of this journey was a Mr. George Bemis, equally unseasoned. Bemis was the proud owner of an old Allen "pepperbox" revolver. The three of them, shooting in unison, were never able to bring down a jack rabbit, and would have been in serious trouble had they met warlike Indians or stagecoach robbers.

But life seemed wonderful as they sped westward behind six spirited horses, sprawled comfortably amid the great load of overland mail, smoking serenely and telling yarns. This was no common nor light experience on which they were embarking, but a journey of the Argonauts in quest of the Golden Fleece. Orion had been promised a salary of $1,800 a year; but more important, he would be the second highest official in the territory and would be acting

Governor in the Governor's absence. Sam's prospects seemed even more glamorous. When not serving as secretary to the Secretary, he fully intended to amass a huge fortune for all of them by mining the silver outcroppings of Nevada.

In any event, they were now traversing the great westward trail—the path of promise that still lured mankind to the farthest reaches of the continent, a road first traced by daring explorers, mountain men in buckskin, 49'ers and Mormons following Brigham Young to the "New Jerusalem" in Utah.

"It was a superb summer morning" as the driver cracked his whip and the horses swung into their stride. "All the landscape was brilliant with sunshine. There was a freshness and breeziness too, and an exhilarating sense of emancipation from all sorts of cares and responsibilities . . . We were spinning along through Kansas, and in the course of an hour and a half were fairly abroad on the great plains."* For a time the land billowed "like the stately heave and swell of the ocean's bosom after a storm." But

---

*This quotation, like many of the others on the following pages of Chapter 5, is taken from Mark Twain's *Roughing It,* a lively account of his years in the West.

presently it leveled out to stretch away "seven hundred miles" almost as smooth as a floor.

Above them, exposed to the weather, rode the Driver and the Conductor—very important personages at the frequent relay stations where the teams were exchanged for fresh horses. Sleep was easy for the passengers on this level terrain where the swaying of the stage was like the pleasant motion of a boat on a summer sea. Except for the breaking of a brace on a drizzly night, no discomfort marred these early miles of the journey. Soon they were passing through Marysville, and over the Big Blue River, and were angling northwest into Nebraska. Sam Clemens was delighted when they caught their first glimpse of sagebrush. He liked the pungent smell of its gray-green leaves so like the garden sage he knew at home; and he praised its hard, dry wood for the cheerful campfires it furnished, followed by glowing coals for roasting meat.

When the August days were too hot, the three men stripped to their underwear for comfort, pulled back the curtains of the stage and enjoyed the breeze. By sundown they were ready for sleep, rushing along through the cool, dark immensity of the night. Now and then they were startled awake as the stage plunged down a bank into a stream and up the other side. By morning when they reached some relay station for yet another change of horses, they were always famished for breakfast—poor as the fare often proved to be.

Fifty-six hours and 300 miles out of St. Joseph, they crossed the Platte River at Fort Kearney and realized that they were getting well into the West. Soon they were seeing prairie dog villages and their first antelope. For many miles the trail now followed the Platte, and its branch the North Platte, westward into what would one day be the State of Wyoming. Coyotes howled at night. Pony Express riders flashed by, carrying letters at $5 each, 1,900 miles from Sacramento to St. Joseph, oblivious of storms and alkali dust, and of Indian bullets whizzing past their ears—little men, lightly clad for speed, and often completely unarmed—some of the bravest men in the world.

Once in the night they heard murderous cries. Shots rang out, but they sped on. Once they met a company of soldiers returning from a brisk skirmish with 400 Indians. On another occasion they overtook a band of Mormons moving slowly toward Utah—weary men, women, and children driving their cattle and plodding endlessly down the dusty trail beside their covered wagons.

Westward, ever westward along the North Platte and then the Sweetwater, until at last through the hot, dry August air they saw, shimmering in the distance, the snow-capped mountains! In another day or two they were in the heart of the Rockies headed for South Pass and the Continental Divide. "We had been climbing, patiently climbing for days and nights together—and about us was gathered a convention of Nature's kings that stood ten, twelve, and even thirteen thousand feet high." How small by comparison now seemed those heights of Sam's boyhood, Holliday's Hill and Lover's Leap!

When they reached the highest point of the pass they came to a spring with two outlets, sending rivulets in one direction toward the Gulf of Mexico and the other toward the Gulf of California—feeding, eventually, the Atlantic and the Pacific with its small contributions. Sam put a leaf on the stream flowing eastward. He sent with it "a mental message for the friends at home . . . But I put no stamp on it and it was held for postage somewhere."

The party rested for two days in Brigham Young's busy capital, Salt Lake City. The houses appeared remarkably neat, set in lush gardens, vineyards, and orchards, irrigated by crystal streams diverted from the mountains.

Onward rolled the stage, across alkali flats, mountain passes, and strange little rivers which began at the snow line and disappeared mysteriously in the sands of the desert. They had now crossed the border into "Washoe" (as Nevada was affectionately known to the ranchers and miners). On the twentieth day they wheeled with a flourish into the drab street of saloons, small stores, and frame houses which constituted the heart of Carson City, capital of the territory. A gunfight was in progress in the street, drawing mild interest from the loafers along the board sidewalks. One contestant rode away bleeding from several wounds, while the other returned to mending his whip. Meanwhile a "Washoe Zephyr" was picking up everything loose and sailing it into the next county. Such desolation! And such a wind!

"Seriously," says Sam, "a Washoe wind is by no means a trifling matter. It blows flimsy houses down, lifts shingle roofs occasionally, rolls up tin ones like sheet music, now and then blows a stage coach over and spills the passengers; and tradition says the reason there are so many bald people there is that the wind blows the hair off their heads while they are looking skyward after their hats."

Orion's spirits fell a little when he learned that his office, as well as his home, would be one small bedroom in Bridget O'Flannigan's boardinghouse. However, he fared better than his brother Sam, who soon discovered that *his* luxurious quarters consisted of a single cot, ranged among thirteen others, in the attic above. There might be glory ahead for Orion in his appointment, and a fortune in silver for Sam if he could find it, but with the Washoe Zephyr shaking the boardinghouse as a terrier shakes a rat, Nevada seemed a bit bleak and barren to the usually optimistic brothers who had come so far by stagecoach to reach this "land of endless promise."

Carson City was to be Sam Clemens' home base, and point of departure for various adventures, from August 1861 to midsummer of the next year. The territorial government of Nevada furnished enough paperwork to keep Orion mildly occupied for a few hours each day, but provided neither the excitement nor the incentive to tie Sam to a dull desk.

Sam had spent nine diligent and profitless years setting type. He had faithfully guided river steamers on the New Orleans–St. Louis run for an additional four years. He was now nearly twenty-six years old, without having had a full month of relaxation since he was eleven years of age. In his quiet, soft-spoken way, he was experiencing and expressing a long-delayed moment of rebellion.

First evidence of his rebellion was a change of dress. The recently immaculate river pilot now acquired cowhide boots, a slouch hat and the other rough but comfortable clothing of the western miners. He began to grow a "ruck of ruddy curls" on his chin. For several days he lounged around Carson City, leaning against the buildings and gazing at the motley population. Soon, to a favored few, he began telling amusing stories in his slow drawl, pausing for effect, nailing down his unexpected conclusions. In less than three weeks he was one of the best-known and best-liked men in town.

His second small rebellion was to share with a friend an utterly idle outing on nearby Lake Tahoe, sleeping under blankets beneath the stars, drifting in a little boat for endless hours on water so clear that every trout and boulder could be seen eighty feet below the surface. His description of this trip in letters home to his mother and Pamela are among the first evidences that Samuel Langhorne Clemens might one day become a really talented writer.

Back in Carson City, with autumn adding a breath of frost to the mountain air, Sam began to realize that his vacation was over, and that he must now think seriously of that fortune he was always intending to make for himself and his family. News of an unbelievable silver strike in the Humboldt region around Unionville fired Sam and some of his friends with silver fever. Cartloads of solid silver bricks passed through Carson City every day. Fortunes were being made and lost almost overnight. The entire population was floating deliriously on hopes which seemed so tangible that every man was certain he eventually would be a millionaire.

Sam was soon organizing a prospecting party consisting of himself, two young lawyers, and a sixty-year-old blacksmith named Ballou. The three greenhorns and one veteran purchased two ancient horses, a wagon, and 1,800 pounds of provisions and mining equipment. On a chilly December afternoon they left Carson City at a snail's pace, the men walking, and frequently helping to push the wagon.

It took fifteen days and nights of frigid misery to traverse the 200 miles, a journey they could scarcely have endured save for their visions of mountains of pure silver which seemed to be shining not far ahead.

Unionville consisted of "eleven cabins and a liberty pole." The exhausted prospecting party "built a small, rude cabin in the side of the crevice and roofed it with canvas." Sam was as high-strung as an Indian pony, curious as a catamount, eager as a beaver to be about his serious quest of finding his fortune. As soon as possible he wandered off alone to discover his silver mine. On that very first excursion he found in the gravel of a little creek a rich deposit of yellow, shining scales. Not silver, Sam thought, but gold—virgin gold! He filled his sack with pounds of this treasure and returned to the camp, gloating.

Sam tantalized his partners for a time, reveling deliciously in his secret, until at last they demanded an explanation. Then, as they gathered around him in the candlelight, he tossed his glittering hoard before them. The two young lawyers were overwhelmed with excitement. But the blacksmith, Ballou, was no fool. He was an experienced prospector for both silver and gold. And he swiftly dismissed this pile of "gold" as nothing but rubbish, a little mica from shattered granite and not worth "ten cents an acre."

Many wearying days now followed during which no member of the party discovered an ounce of silver ore. But at last they found a ledge of rock slanting into the mountain which even Ballou agreed had traces of silver in it. Immediately they named their mine "Monarch of the Mountains," and posted the following proclamation:

NOTICE

We the undersigned claim three claims, of three hundred feet each (and one for discovery) on this silver-bearing quartz lead or lode, extending north and south from this notice, with all its dips, spurs and angles, variations and sinuosities, together with fifty feet of ground on either side for working the same.

Each of the party signed this document, and one of the lawyers was careful to make a duplicate copy to be filed at the Mining Recorder's office in town.

They were fabulously rich—or so everyone except the blacksmith believed. He continued to remain surprisingly unexcited. Sam and the two attorneys retained their optimism for several days as they toiled, an inch at a time, down through the flintlike ledge, picking, shoveling, blasting—laboring until they were numb with fatigue and cold. Sam had always enjoyed digging for treasure around Hannibal. But in Missouri one could at least choose soft loam, or at worst gravel or clay. Here in Nevada there seemed to be nothing but rock as hard as cast iron. One week of this was enough for Sam. A few more days discouraged the others. They had chipped a twelve-foot shaft into the quartz, with no indication that the ore would ever prove rich enough to take to the stamping mill.

Back in Carson City after an arduous trek beset by flood, blizzards, and near loss of life, Sam was briefly despondent. Then he heard fresh rumors of silver strikes in the Esmeralda region near the California border. Off he went again, in the dead of winter, to experience several months of similar hopes and disappointments. Once, very briefly, Sam and his new partner, Calvin H. Higbie—a gentle, goodhearted but ill-educated giant—thought they had made their fortune. They had discovered a "blind lead"—that is, a vein of ore which at no place reaches the surface. But a series of unfortunate coincidences invalidated their ten-day claim, and they lost to other prospectors the "millions" they had hoped to make from the Wide West Mine.

Sam, sick at heart, took a "villainously hard job" in a quartz stamping mill, at $10 a week. After his first week's wages he realized that he was forever disillusioned with hard-rock silver mining and must swiftly find some other means of making a living.

More as a pastime than as a profession, Sam had been writing newsletters from Esmeralda to the liveliest newspaper in Nevada, the Virginia City *Territorial Enterprise*. And just when his luck as a miner was at its lowest ebb, he received an unbelievable offer from Joseph T. Goodman, the proprietor of that paper. Goodman thought Sam's letters were top-notch journalism. Very deliberately he offered $25 a week to serve as the paper's "city editor." Sam's decision to accept this offer was one of the great turning points in his career.

Sam hiked through the mountains for 130 miles to the thriving silver town of Virginia City, perched on a series of rocky terraces on the side of Mount Davidson. He could not get across the main thoroughfare, on which the paper's new building was located, because of the traffic jam. Quartz wagons bearing silver ore for the stamping mills rumbled by, stirring the August dust. Fire laddies in their bright red shirts, lodge brothers in their gaudy regalia, and other sorrowing citizens were marching behind a hearse carrying the corpse of a prominent saloon-keeper recently shot in a gun battle. The fancy carriages of mining nabobs and their overdressed ladies jostled for right of way with Wells Fargo stage-coaches, crammed with passengers and silver bullion destined for California. From outlying ranches there arrived several wagons loaded with hay (worth at this moment $250 a ton). And now to add to the throng, more than 1,000 miners started streaming from holes in the ground as the work force changed shifts at the rich Ophir and Gould and Curry mines. In short, here was the normal traffic of a busy day during "flush times" in Virginia City.

When Sam finally managed to cross the street to the *Enterprise* office he was already impressed, bewildered, and fatigued. This town was *something*! It made Carson City, the territorial capital, look like the rag-town it was.

"I was a rusty-looking city editor, I am free to confess—coatless, slouch hat, blue woolen shirt, pantaloons stuffed into boot tops, whiskered half down to the waist."

But Sam could change his costume at least as rapidly as he changed his dramatic role in life. Soon he was as sharply dressed as all the other editors and reporters in town. In only one respect did his attire differ from theirs. They followed the universal fashion of wearing at least one revolver. Sam, who had "never had occasion to kill anybody, nor ever felt a desire to do so," went unarmed.

Young Clemens, who had been a pilot among pilots and a miner among miners, now became a reporter among reporters—probably the best "city editor" who ever recorded the rowdy life of Virginia City. Deep within, he remained the sensitive person he had always been. But superficially he hardened himself to the ceaseless, brutal killings—covering all such episodes with flashes of color, pathos, or grim humor. He picked up news from immigrant trains moving through the town; wrote front-page stories on every new silver strike; dashed off quips, burlesques, and satirical attacks upon rival journalists— in short lived and reported the rough-and-ready life of one of the widest-open mining towns the world has ever known.

"Down cellar" beneath the town were more than thirty miles of wide tunnels crisscrossing the fabulous Comstock Lode. "Up stairs" were many billiard parlors, gambling halls, theaters, saloons, and jails all doing a land-office business. The cemetery was also a busy place—"the first 26 graves" occupied by men who had been murdered. Sam found it relatively easy to fill his two columns each day with the sort of news that always fascinated Virginia City.

Sam's salary was soon boosted to $40 a week, paid in gold. But Clemens considered this a trifling sum since, on the side, he was rapidly accumulating mining stock. Friends gave each other "feet" in various mines. And a "foot" of a rich vein of silver, worth a few dollars one week, might soar to hundreds and even thousands of dollars a few weeks later. Other "feet" selling for hundreds of dollars might sink to zero when the mine proved worthless. In this madly fluctuating market, no one knew from one month to the next whether he was rich or bankrupt. Everyone was constantly intoxicated with dreams of millions; and most of the town was also intoxicated with whisky.

Sam Clemens knew two teamsters who accepted,

in lieu of a $300 debt, a portion of a silver mine. Less than a year afterward they were making $100,000 a year apiece from their small investment.

"In the early days a poverty-stricken Mexican, who lived in a canyon directly back of Virginia City, had a stream of water as large as a man's wrist trickling from the hillside on his premises. The Ophir Company segregated a hundred feet of their mine and traded it to him for the stream of water. The hundred feet proved to be the richest part of the entire mine." Four years later its market value was $1,500,000.

To a certain extent Sam was carried away by this madness, but he remained an excellent reporter and did his work faithfully and courageously.

He showed courage, for instance, in walking the streets of Virginia City without a weapon. He was almost recklessly brave in his descents into collapsing mines, far beneath the earth, to see for himself how the interlaced beams, reaching as high as a church steeple, were slowly being crushed as the roof came down. Most fearless of all was his public defense of the humble Chinese—those industrious and uncomplaining souls who washed the clothing of the miners, grew excellent vegetables in the rocky soil, and meekly accepted the beatings and stonings of the hoodlums of the town.

Early in 1863 Sam realized that his much-quoted, and often-reprinted stories deserved some tag of identification. Many of the other reporters had pseudonyms which in time became more widely known than their real names. Sam talked to his friend and employer Joe Goodman about this matter.

"I'd like to sign my articles from now on, Joe."

"A good idea. What name have you chosen?"

"Mark Twain!"

"Mark Twain? I rather like that, Sam. But what does it mean?"

"It's from my river days—the cry of the leadsman when he finds a safe two fathoms of water—Mark Twain! Mark Twain!"*

---

*The theory that the pseudonym "Mark Twain" was first used by Isaiah Sellers, an old-time pilot on the Mississippi, for letters which he wrote to New Orleans papers, has been sharply questioned by several critics and researchers. Oddly enough it was Mark Twain himself who gave currency to this origin of the name. Until a deeper study of the problem has been made we should all remain open-minded on the question.

"Go ahead and use it, Sam. Mark Twain might be famous some day—at least here in the West."

It injected new life into his writing to see his pen name attached to all his articles. It put more zest into his mining stories, more humor and vigor into his hilarious accounts of the political shenanigans in Carson City. Maybe Joe Goodman's faith in him was justified—possibly he really *was* destined for more creative tasks than filling two columns a day for the *Territorial Enterprise*.

It is ironical that a man so fundamentally gentle as Mark Twain, a man who always went unarmed, should have ended his days in Virginia City in the manner that he did.

During the absence of Goodman on a holiday, Clemens was elevated to editorship of the paper. Besides his usual stint he now must also fill several columns on the editorial page. This proved an almost impossible additional assignment. One day he wrote a long article on William Shakespeare. The next day he copied whole pages from an encyclopedia that lay at hand. Gradually he became desperate for copy.

Then he remembered the timeworn custom of attacking the opposition press—a trick that had worked successfully in Hannibal, and which constantly enlivened journalism in Virginia City.

Sam wrote a sizzler about his friend Laird, proprietor of the *Union*. Laird retaliated with a similar sizzler that went whizzing past Sam's ears like a bullet from a six-shooter. Sam answered Laird; Laird answered Sam—and all was as merry as a Washoe Zephyr!

According to the custom of the day, when a rival editor went too far, the most aggrieved party was supposed to send a challenge to fight a duel. When Laird was so impolite as to disregard completely this courtesy, two of Sam's friends on the *Enterprise* took matters into their own hands and sent a challenge to Laird in Sam's name. Laird didn't answer the first challenge, nor the second. But the *Enterprise* faction finally "overdid it" and Laird accepted.

Mark Twain was ashamed of this episode and kept it from the public for many years. But when writing his *Autobiography* he put it all down as he remembered it:

"The boys were jubilant beyond expression. They helped me make my will, which was another discomfort—and I already had enough. Then they took me home. I didn't sleep any—didn't want to sleep. I had plenty of things to think about and less than four hours to do it in—because five o'clock was the hour appointed for the tragedy and I should have to use up one hour—beginning at four—in practicing with the revolver and finding out which end of it to level at the adversary. At four we went down into a little gorge about a mile from town and borrowed a barn door for a mark—borrowed it of a man who was over in California on a visit."

Steve Gillis, Sam's friend and second in the affray, said that Laird was a pretty thin target. So he leaned a fence rail against the barn door and asked Sam to hit it. Sam emptied his revolver several times, never touching the rail and feeling fortunate when he could hit the barn door.

Meanwhile, from the next ravine, came the reports of other shots where Laird, an excellent marksman, was also practicing with his pistol. This did not encourage Sam Clemens, who thought he was watching his last sunrise and wondered how he had ever allowed himself to become tangled in such a mess.

Steve was growing impatient with Sam's marksmanship. He borrowed the revolver for a moment, pointed at a bird no larger than a sparrow perched in the sagebrush about thirty yards away, and shot its head off. At just this moment Laird and his second came over the hill to see how Sam was doing with his marksmanship. They saw Steve run to pick up the bird, and were immediately curious.

Laird's second asked, "Who did that?"

Before Sam could answer, Steve spoke up and said quite calmly, "Clemens did it."

Laird's second said, "Why that is wonderful! How far off was that bird?"

Steve said, "Oh, not far—about thirty yards."

The second said, "Well, that is astonishing shooting. How often can he do that?"

Steve said languidly, "Oh, about four times out of five!"

There was a hurried conference in the Laird camp, with much animated discussion. After a few moments the opposition politely bade Sam and Steve farewell. Laird went home "a little tottery on his legs," and soon sent back "a note in his own hand declining to fight a duel," on any terms whatever.

Sam's life and "honor" had been saved. Steve had done his best to promote the duel, and then to frighten off Sam's opponent. But both of these easy winners now faced a completely unsuspected danger. Unknown to either, a new law had just been enacted in Carson City which made it a crime to send a challenge—a crime which might net both Sam and Steve as much as two years in jail. These two friends decided that they were rather tired of Nevada—a bleak, windy, desolate country. They agreed that there were greener pastures just over the mountains in California. Within twenty-four hours they had packed their few belongings and were aboard a Wells Fargo stagecoach climbing the snowy Sierra for a view down the other side into a region of perpetual sunshine.

It was spring of the year 1864 when Sam Clemens reached San Francisco—but in truth it is always spring in that city beside its spacious bay. Sam enjoyed for a time "a butterfly idleness." He fell in love with "the most cordial and sociable city in the Union. After the sagebrush and alkali deserts of Washoe, San Francisco was paradise."

This treasure-seeker who had drilled, shoveled, and blasted so futilely in the Humboldt and Esmeralda mines, had subsequently acquired in Virginia City enough mining stock to make him a wealthy man, if the boom continued. But for each boom in the world there is usually a bust, and it was soon apparent to thousands of speculators that a large proportion of the Nevada mines were completely worthless. Mining shares fell precipitously that year until many were as valueless as Confederate money. Sam Clemens had believed himself to be worth nearly $100,000. He now found that after paying his current debts he had less than $50 in his pocket.

Orion could be of no assistance to Sam in this crisis. "Acting Governor" Clemens had made so many political blunders that he had ruined his chances of ever again holding public office. For the rest of his life Orion would be almost completely dependent upon Sam's generosity.

"Mark Twain" now took a job on the San Francisco *Morning Call*, where Steve Gillis labored as a typesetter. Sam's work was "fearful drudgery" from early morning to late at night: homicides, weddings, and funerals from dawn to dusk; and, after the evening meal, "six theaters, one after the other: seven nights in the week, three hundred and sixty-five nights in the year."

Sam finally parted company with the *Call* and for a time wrote sketches for Bret Harte's magazine, the

Californian, at the then-excellent rate of $12 a story. He also became San Francisco correspondent for his old paper, the *Territorial Enterprise,* and in his dispatches, lashed out so fearlessly at the corruption of the San Francisco police department that he was warned to leave town if he valued his life.

Clemens took a long vacation in the peaceful Tuolumne Hills, living in the comfortable cabin of Jim Gillis (brother of Steve)—a pocket miner working over the abandoned gold diggings of that once-rich region. Sam found no precious metal, but he did pick up several stories which later found their way into his books. One of these tales he entitled "The Celebrated Jumping Frog of Calaveras County." In a letter to his mother, Sam accurately described this yarn as "a villainous backwoods sketch"—but it was the beginning of his fame.

His trouble with the police department eventually vanished into the San Francisco mists. Rested and refreshed from his sojourn in the hills, Sam decided to rejoin civilization.

"I returned from the 'pocket' mines to San Francisco and wrote letters to the Virginia *Enterprise* for a while and was then sent to the Sandwich [Hawaiian] Islands by the Sacramento *Union* . . .

While I was in Honolulu the survivors of the clipper
Hornet . . . arrived, mere skin and bone relics, after
a passage of forty-three days in an open boat on ten
days' provisions; and I worked all day and all night
and produced a full and complete account of the
matter and flung it aboard a schooner which had already cast off. It was the only full account that went
to California, and the *Union* paid me tenfold the
current rates for it."

Sam had a carefree time in Hawaii wandering
happily over the islands on foot or on horseback. He
was constantly delighted by the tropical blaze of
flowers, the little cascades gleaming like silver rib-
bons against the dark green foliage of the mountains. Missionaries had begun to dress the natives in
ugly cotton garments, but these were flung aside
with innocent abandon as men, women, and children dashed into the surf or plunged into the clear
pools below the waterfalls. The music, laughter, and
freedom of Hawaii soon cured this visitor of any
sadness or bitterness he may have felt in San
Francisco. The world was again filled with good life,
to the brim!

In his *Autobiography* he says:

"After about four or five months I returned to California to find myself about the best-known honest man on the Pacific coast. Thomas McGuire, proprietor of several theaters, said that now was the time to make my fortune—strike while the iron was hot—break into the lecture field! I did it. I announced a lecture on the Sandwich Islands, closing the advertisement with the remark: 'Admission one dollar; doors open at half past seven, the trouble begins at eight.' A true prophecy. The trouble certainly did begin at eight, when I found myself in front of the only audience I had ever faced, for the fright which pervaded me from head to foot was paralyzing. It lasted two minutes and was as bitter as death; the memory of it is indestructible, but it had its compensations, for it made me immune from timidity before audiences for all time to come."

Sam's fears on this occasion proved groundless. These were his friends; and, as he began in his slow, inimitable drawl to tell amusing and touching stories of his trip to the Islands, a rumble of amiable laughter shook the well-packed house. The evening was a complete and resounding success—the first of many hundreds of such evenings; for although Sam never liked lecturing, he became the greatest attraction of the American lecture platform during the next three decades.

The aimless boy of Hannibal, Missouri, was adding to his many professions: he was an accomplished typesetter; a river pilot knowing the Mississippi between St. Louis and New Orleans; a miner who could at least differentiate gold and silver ore from "fool's gold" and mica; a newspaper reporter and correspondent, and now—apparently—a lecturer able to sweep audiences from their feet and roll them in the aisles. He lectured in all the major towns on the western slopes of the mountains, and was welcomed back to Virginia City with a noisy display of Washoe hospitality.

Only one incident marred his return to Nevada. Several practical jokers—all "old friends"—donned masks and waylaid him in a lonely place on a cold, dark night. Sam knew it was a joke, but when it had been prolonged until they were all chilled to the bone, the revolvers still pointed menacingly at his head, Sam grew a little weary of the fun. He determined, then and there, that practical joking was a very low, cruel form of humor and he never again in his life played such a prank on anyone, nor accepted one played on himself without showing a trace of temper. Evidently he was beginning to reach maturity.

The East was now beckoning this author of increasing fame. The voyage from San Francisco to the Isthmus of Panama, across that steaming strip of jungle—and on to New York aboard a ship infected with cholera was scarcely a pleasure cruise. But it was exciting to see the great City of New York once again and presently to hold in his hands his first published book—a handsome little cloth and gold edition of his *Jumping Frog*—containing that tale and several other sketches. Villainous backwoods story or not, all America was laughing over it, and Mark Twain could only gaze with wonder at his first little volume. To his incredulous joy and amazement he was now the author of a book—the first of many that would soon extend into an entire shelf—the most notable and beloved set of volumes any single American writer would produce during the latter half of the nineteenth century. Mark Twain had brought wealth more precious than gold nuggets from his six years in the West—he had brought the immortal substance from which literature is made, and the vital nucleus of a new career.

6

THE MINIATURE
AND THE GIRL HERSELF
(1867–1870)

Throughout his life Mark Twain was a restless man, continuously vibrating with curiosity and creative energy. He had a passion to learn, to see the world, to write entertaining books and to make a fortune. He had gone west, and west again, as far as the Hawaiian Islands. Now he wanted to see Europe and the countries surrounding the Mediterranean—eastward this time, as far as the *Quaker City* would take him.

The *Quaker City* was an ocean-going side-wheeler, a quaint little transatlantic steamer of that era, and one of the first excursion ships designed to accommodate Americans wishing to improve themselves with foreign travel. The cost of a five-month cruise was $1,250—rather more than Mark Twain had in his pocket. But by arranging with two newspapers to publish his travel letters, he soon had the fare. The *Alta California* would purchase the bulk of these dispatches, fifty-three articles at $20 each. The *New York Tribune* was to buy six others.

As the sailing date approached, Twain was eager for the departure. While picking up his ticket, he asked if there were to be any celebrities aboard, and was startled and gratified to learn that he himself was the principal attraction. The sixty-six pilgrims were largely graybeards and elderly ladies whose conversation was far from sprightly. But Sam did discover a few interesting companions including his roommate Dan Slote, the motherly and quick-witted Mrs. Fairbanks from Cleveland, and a gay young blade of eighteen named Charles Langdon from Elmira, New York.

To these and a few other favored passengers he read his rollicking letters, written as the cruise progressed—reports on the trip which were breezy, amusing, and sometimes outrageous—the varied reactions of a group of culture-hungry Americans amid the cathedrals and art galleries of France and Italy and the shrines and villages of the arid Holy Land. Seen through Mark Twain's sharp eyes, the happenings on shipboard and ashore were continually entertaining.

But much more than a series of travel sketches re-
sulted from this historic journey. One day, when the
ship was at anchor in the Bay of Smyrna, "Charlie"
Langdon showed Sam Clemens a miniature of his
adored sister, Olivia, a beautiful and serious young
woman with dark hair and large dark eyes. Sam fell
in love with that picture; it haunted him throughout
the rest of the cruise, and he made a firm resolve to
see Livy Langdon herself at the first possible opportunity.

When the *Quaker City* returned safely to New
York in November, Sam had not long to wait. Jervis
Langdon and his wife made it a custom each year
to enjoy the Christmas holidays at the fashionable
million-dollar St. Nicholas Hotel located between
Spring and Broome streets on Broadway. The St.
Nicholas had a feature that was quite remarkable
for its time, a central-heating plant that piped hot
air to every room. Its lobbies and dining rooms, re-
splendent by gaslight, catered to a select clientele—
the women in rustling silks and crinolines, the
bewhiskered men in well-tailored Prince Alberts.

Langdon, who was a wealthy coal dealer from
Elmira, always took one of the large suites for himself and his wife, their beloved and overly protected

daughter Olivia, their adopted daughter Susan, and their debonair only son, Charlie, who had been Sam's companion on the *Quaker City*.

When Charlie brought Sam Clemens to meet his interesting but slightly formidable family on the blustery evening of December 27, 1867, he had not the slightest idea that he was playing Cupid. Olivia was much too good for Sam, in fact too good for any man, as the whole Langdon family knew. But perhaps they noticed more than gaslight shining in Sam's eyes when he first gazed upon this "sweet and timid and lovely young girl." Her black hair was parted in the middle and drawn back in a neat chignon, severe but classic. Her skin and complexion were delicate and petal-like. Her large, dark eyes held Sam spellbound; and when she began talking, he was amazed to hear so much common sense, keen intelligence and charm, all on the small pink tongue of one shy girl.

What if Jervis Langdon, with his muttonchop whiskers, did seem the most protective papa who ever scowled at an eager suitor? What if her mother was a prayerful, Bible-reading teetotaler, and every inch an Elmira matron? Neither of these potential stumbling blocks in the path of true love could discourage Sam Clemens, who knew immediately that he had met the only girl he had ever wanted to marry.

After a many-course dinner at the St. Nicholas, Sam was taken by the family to hear Charles Dickens in a reading he was giving that night at Steinway Hall. Sam spent most of his time watching Livy—but he did glance now and then at the other attraction of the evening, Dickens, who was wearing a black velvet coat with a flaming red flower in his buttonhole. Mark Twain, who was rapidly becoming a famous lecturer himself, admired Dickens' calm and easy manner in holding so large an audience with such a simple device as reading a dramatic passage from *David Copperfield*.

Sam waited impatiently throughout the five days, which decorum decreed was the minimum, before he again might ask to call on Olivia. On New Year's Day, Livy was helping a friend named Mrs. Berry receive callers at her town house. Sam is said to have arrived at 10 A.M. and stayed for thirteen hours. During that long, enchanted day he had many moments with Olivia. And, shy though she was, she told this attentive young man a few things about herself and her life in Elmira.

Livy was twenty-two at this time; Sam thirty-two. She had suffered a skating accident at sixteen, and for two years had been confined to her bed, this being one of the reasons for the excessively protective attitude of her parents. For the last four years she had been able to walk, but only short distances. Fail and delicate though she seemed, she was a woman of zest and warmth and courage, as Sam was to learn in the years that lay ahead. But with a growing sense of desperation Sam contemplated the great gulf that lay between them—he a rough-hewn Westerner and she a hothouse orchid from a sternly religious family of wealth and culture. Livy, too, was aware of their many differences. She was secretly fascinated, although a trifle frightened. It would not be a swift or an easy courtship (as they both realized).

Sam broadly hinted to Charlie that he wanted an invitation to visit the Langdon home in Elmira. But Olivia's brother was becoming cautious; and there were other reasons why this visit was delayed for eight long months.

Early in 1868 the American Publishing Company of Hartford, Connecticut, made Mark Twain a tempting offer to publish a book composed of his rewritten travel sketches; a book to be entitled *The*

Innocents Abroad. The publisher desired a completed manuscript as soon as possible. Clemens was more than willing, but discovered to his chagrin that the *Alta California* had copyrighted his travel letters and had no intention of letting him use the material for a book. Furious at this "chicanery," Sam was soon aboard ship on his way to the Pacific coast. Upon arrival, he went directly to the *Alta* office, where his logic and charm prevailed with his old friend Colonel McComb. Free now to write his book, he began almost immediately revising the script.

While in the West he also made several successful lectures, his first in San Francisco grossing $1,600 in gold. Richer by many dollars, he returned to the East, where in late July he delivered his manuscript, and made his acquaintance with the delightful little city of Hartford, Connecticut, which would later become his home. In August he found himself free for the first time to visit the Langdons in Elmira.

Despite his growing fame, Sam Clemens was a trifle overwhelmed during the first visit. Having been met at the railroad station by the coachman, he was soon being taken up the neatly kept drive through the beautiful grounds surrounding the big Langdon home. He noticed the conservatory where flowers were grown "mostly for funerals," Sam thought. The many narrow windows were curtained by such heavy draperies that the visitor wondered how any ray of sunshine ever entered. Once inside, however, Sam began to realize that the Langdon mansion was far from forbidding. There were many shelves of books; a piano around which the family gathered to sing hymns; flowers, beautiful furniture, and an atmosphere of love and graceful living.

Sam added the much-needed sunshine to this conservative conviviality, and soon found that the Langdons were not the ogres he had imagined. He was astonished to discover, for instance, that they entertained in their home many "liberals" of the day, including the Black orator Frederick Douglass, and that they were quietly contributing thousands of dollars to help educate Blacks and poor Whites in the South. In addition to this, Jervis Langdon had a twinkle of humor hidden deep within his formidable exterior.

Mildly encouraged by the hospitality of his hosts, Sam proposed to Olivia, and was promptly refused. The next day he proposed again, and was again refused. She said, in gentle but firm reproof, that he might address her as "sister" in his letters, and she in turn would call him "brother"—but nothing further could be hoped for—now, or at any time in the future.

Sam was in despair, but never ceased to be determined. He went west to see his mother and Pamela in St. Louis, and to them confessed his love for this unobtainable girl. These women, who had given him comfort all his life, comforted him again and encouraged him in his suit. And now began the series of 184 courting letters, which Livy would treasure in a little green box—letters filled with restrained passion, with the agony of separation, with promises, pleas, and pledges of devotion to his aloof but alluring "sister." Thinking he sensed a slightly warmer tone in one of Livy's latest missives, Sam rushed back to Elmira.

The elder Langdons did not receive him quite as graciously as before, and did not react with the same sympathetic laughter when he told droll stories. This time he was not complimented on his fine tenor voice when he joined in singing hymns at the piano. And when he again proposed to Livy, her answer still was "No!"

Sam was beginning to feel that never since his

silver-mining days had he labored so diligently with such negligible results.

When his evening train was nearly due, he said good-bye to the family grouped on the front porch, and with Charlie climbed into the democrat wagon (which was certainly not the best equipage in the coach house). Charlie and Sam were sitting on the rear seat, which for some reason was not locked in place. Barney the coachman touched up the horses. The wagon leaped forward, throwing Charlie and Sam over the stern, backward.

Years later in his *Autobiography*, Mark Twain recalled:

"In the darkness the red bud of fire on the end of [Charlie's] cigar described a curve through the air which I can see yet. This was the only visible thing in all that gloomy scenery. I struck exactly on the top of my head and stood up that way for a moment, then crumbled down to the earth unconscious. It was a very good unconsciousness for a person who had not rehearsed the part. It was a cobblestone gutter and they had been repairing it. My head struck in a dish formed by the conjunction of four cobblestones. That depression was half full of fresh new sand and this made a competent cushion . . . I got not a bruise. I was not even jolted. Nothing was the matter with me at all.

"Charlie was considerably battered, but in his solicitude for me he was substantially unaware of it. The whole family swarmed out . . . It was very pleasant to hear the pitying remarks trickling around over me. That was one of the happiest half dozen moments of my life . . ."

Sam was carried into the parlor and placed in a comfortable chair. The family physician was called; and, while the Langdons anxiously awaited his arrival, Livy began rubbing Sam's head. "It was very delightful, those manipulations. So comforting, so enchanting . . ."

Naturally there was no question now of putting their injured visitor aboard the train. He must remain and rest until he was "well enough to travel." Sam was charming and quite pitiable during the three days that followed. He was convinced that he was making some headway with Livy. And she, in turn, was beginning to admit to herself that she was feeling a trifle closer than a sister to this redheaded, impulsive suitor.

Sam, however, was taking no chances. He arranged his lecture schedule so that frequently he was in the Elmira area. He continued to pour out a Niagara of letters, proposing, and being refused, and proposing once again. He even went so far as to let Livy try to "reform" him. He promised to pray every day, attend church, and read the Bible. He said he would curb his salty language, sweeten his vocabulary, and refrain from profanity. As a last resort he made the final sacrifice, saying he would reduce his 300 cigars a month to thirty, if it killed him.

Sam's letters to Jervis Langdon were full of business zeal and common sense—just the type to impress a big coal dealer who thought Sam was a delightful rascal, but scarcely the solid mate for his beloved Livy. He spoke of his earnings as a lecturer; the excellent chances for the success of his new book; and his desire to buy a partnership in the *Buffalo Express* so that a steady income would be assured.

On their next meeting, Jervis Langdon gazed long and silently at Sam. He puffed out his muttonchop whiskers, looked Sam squarely in the eye, and asked for eighteen references of character, as many of them as possible from the Far West, where Langdon well imagined that Sam had lived the usual life of the mining camps.

Sam, honestly, did not stack the deck. He might

have given Livy's father a list of sure-fire friends headed by Joe Goodman and Steve Gillis. Instead he offered an objective group of acquaintances, including two ministers of the gospel and not a few miners and journalists who turned out to be practical jokers.

Jervis Langdon received his answers and called Sam into his study. Apparently almost everybody loved Sam, or respected his talents, or found him a boon companion. But not one on the list considered him a good bet as a husband.

"The reading of the letters being finished, there was a good deal of pause and it consisted largely of sadness and solemnity. I couldn't think of anything to say. Mr. Langdon was apparently in the same condition. Finally he raised his handsome head, fixed his clear and candid eye upon me and said: 'What kind of people are these? Haven't you a friend in the world?'

"I said 'Apparently not.'

"Then he said: 'I'll be your friend myself. Take the girl. I know you better than they do.'"

The engagement was sealed on February 4th, 1869, and during the year they had to wait, Sam let Livy gently influence many aspects of his life. She helped correct the proofs for his new book, *The Innocents Abroad*, and so impressed him with her ability as an editor that she became his trusted literary advisor for the next third of a century.

Sam Clemens became increasingly civilized under the tactful guidance of Livy. And Livy became a warmer, more vibrant and enjoyable companion in the healthful sunshine of Sam's love. She, who had seemed so humorless and solemn, began to acquire a delicious sense of humor; and Sam, who had been taught to shake hands in moments of deep emotion, was taught by gentle Livy how to kiss. Theirs was to be one of the great and lasting love affairs.

One final remaining barrier held them apart. Sam, who was supporting his mother and his brother Orion, knew that he now must also support in comfort Livy and any children they might have. On borrowed money he purchased the partnership in the *Buffalo Express;* and he also increased his lecture schedule. Then, quite suddenly, his financial worries disappeared. *The Innocents Abroad* became an overnight best seller, reaching 100,000 purchasers in the first year. His earnings from this source alone soon totaled more than $1,000 a month. Even Jervis Langdon was convinced that his prospective son-in-law would "amount to something." Now Olivia's mother could begin planning, to her heart's content—helping to design the wedding dress, and sending out more than one hundred invitations.

They were married on the second of February, 1870—almost exactly one year after their engagement day. Ill health prevented Sam's mother from attending, but Pamela was among the many guests who gathered in the flower-decked parlors of the Langdon home. A chaperon party of fifteen accompanied the bride and groom to Buffalo, where they were met at the railroad station by a small fleet of horse-drawn sleighs, warm with fur robes and merry with bells.

Sam had directed an associate to rent modest but adequate rooms, and presumably the driver of their sleigh had that new address. But Sam was soon fuming over the odd route they were taking, wandering all through the back streets of Buffalo. Livy was in on the little joke, but she gave no hint; and Sam could only splutter with futile anger. A few minutes later, to Clemens' complete amazement, the sleigh drew up before one of the most beautiful houses in town, located on one of the most fashionable streets.

Hand in hand, Sam and Livy walked up the steps and through the door into a little mansion, ablaze with lights—there to be welcomed by the gay chaperon party. The house was tastefully decorated and furnished; a staff of servants had been hired; and to complete this tale of enchantment, Jervis Langdon— no longer grim—came forward now with a handsome little box. He opened it and handed Sam the keys and the deed to the house.

It was his wedding gift to Sam and Livy.

Sam Clemens' eyes sparkled with affection.

Taking Langdon's hand, he gently drawled, "Whenever you are in Buffalo, if it's twice a year, come right here. Bring your bag and stay over night if you want to. It sha'n't cost you a cent."

Livy was more forthright. She threw her arms about her father and kissed him.

Hours later, when the last guest had gone, Sam and Livy started up the beautiful stairway to their room above, and began their compassionate life together.

7

THE GOLDEN YEARS
(1870–1885)

Four children were born to this happily mated couple. The first was a frail little boy named Langdon who lived less than two years. To comfort them, three lovely little girls arrived: Susy in 1872, Clara in 1874, and Jean in 1880. The earliest memory of each of these daughters was the sound of their father's voice reading aloud episodes from any book he happened to be writing at the time.

Thus Susy, sitting on her mother's lap, was the first child in the world to enjoy the adventures of Tom Sawyer. And both Clara and Jean came along in time to share the excitement of Huck Finn's long voyage down the Mississippi. All three had an excellent sense of humor—particularly the bright and tender Susy with her quick imagination and great admiration for her father.

The family spent almost every summer at Quarry

Farm, which for years had been the Langdon country place. This restful estate three miles east of Elmira was called "Do as you Please Hall." Here the children had cats, ponies, and a playhouse. On very special occasions they were allowed to ride high on a load of fragrant clover hay—three sun-browned little princesses with a coach quite as good as Cinderella's.

Meanwhile their father was busy writing the pages he would read to them later in the afternoon. Mark Twain's study at Quarry Farm was built to resemble the pilot house of a steamship. It had windows on seven of its eight sides, looking out over the peaceful valley of the Chemung River and the blue hills beyond. There in his vine-hung retreat under arching trees, Twain wrote each summer day from about ten in the morning to five in the afternoon. And there in June of 1874 he began one of his finest books, *The Adventures of Tom Sawyer*.

When he was in the mood, words came swiftly to his pen. The first half of *Tom Sawyer* went sailing and surging along like a steamship speeding downstream on a spring flood. He scarcely needed to invent a character or an episode—merely to remember vividly what it was like to be a barefooted boy in a

drowsy river town in those now distant and romantic years before the Civil War—the cave, the island,
his faithful friends and their escapades! For the first
fifteen years of his married life, Twain wrote with
confidence and a joyous sense of creative accom-
plishment. His moments of doubt were always
brushed away by new bursts of energy. If his inspira-
tion failed, as it sometimes did, he had only to put
the manuscript aside for a few months or a few years
and then take it up again and drive through to its
conclusion.

Several of his best books were written in whole
or in part in that octagonal study at Quarry Farm—
"a cosy nest . . . when the storm sweeps down the
remote valley and the lightning flashes behind the
hills beyond, and the rain beats on the roof over my
head, imagine the luxury of it!"

But when the elms began to shower their yellow
leaves upon his study roof, and the far hills flamed
crimson with the maples' fire, it was time each year
to shift the family, the servants, and a vast assortment of luggage to winter quarters. Clemens had
stayed for less than a year and a half in Buffalo,
then, tiring of the newspaper chores which kept him
from his creative writing, he had sold his interest in

the *Buffalo Express* and moved to Hartford. Here, in 1873, Sam and Livy began building a handsome and unusual home of liberal proportions.

This attractive three-story structure of red and yellow brick was designed along lines which startled conservative critics of that era. The windows were large and numerous, to let the whole universe of sunlight and starlight into the twenty spacious rooms. The great living room opened into a small conservatory where flowers ran riot around a central fountain. Turrets and shaded balconies expressed the romance Sam and Livy felt toward each other and toward their home. On the third floor was Sam's quiet study, and the billiard room where he spent hours every day gracefully cueing the ivory balls across the green table, often with a favorite kitten chasing the balls and deflecting them in odd and unintended directions.

It was a house built for love, for gaiety, for Sam and Livy, for the children and for guests—the many interesting people who came and went at their pleasure and were always welcome. Across wide lawns lived the Charles Dudley Warners, Harriet Beecher Stowe and her husband, and other lively literary friends. Reverend "Old Joe" Twichell was a frequent visitor and walking companion. Engraved in brass over the library fireplace were Emerson's cheerful words: *The ornament of a house is the friends who frequent it.*

The luxurious kitchen wing—against all custom —was built toward the street. Sam explained that it saved the carpets, and let the servants see the passing parade without running the length of the house to the front windows.

Here the family spent seventeen happy years, and here Sam began or concluded several of his books.

After the publication of *The Innocents Abroad* a whole series of good and popular volumes flowed from Mark Twain's pen: *Roughing It,* recalling his western years; *The Gilded Age,* a novel written in collaboration with Warner; *The Adventures of Tom Sawyer,* one of his two classics of boyhood; *A Tramp Abroad* telling of his walking tour with "Old Joe" through the Black Forest and the Alps, and *The Prince and the Pauper,* a romantic story of the sixteenth century.

All of these books sold well and earned substantial royalties—but never enough to satisfy Mark Twain. Money flowed through his fingers like water.

He was one of the most generous human beings

the world has ever known. He put several young men through college. No friend in distress ever needed to ask him twice for a loan or gift. Through good times and bad he continued to care for his mother and Orion, sending each $100 a month while they lived. He was particularly generous toward Blacks—whether students or servants. A window washer who came to assist the staff at the Hartford house stayed on indefinitely as the faithful houseman.

Building and maintaining the mansion was expensive; so were the transatlantic trips made by Mark Twain alone, or with his family. Entertaining cost many thousands. Olivia was willing to cut expenses; to live in a small cottage if necessary. She begged her husband to leave the lecture platform; to save himself from his great load of work and worry. Like every really devoted wife, all that she wanted was her husband's happiness, and the quiet family life they could live together.

But Sam had dreams of grandeur in his head. He was still digging for treasure, starry-eyed with hope. He was remotely comparable to his own character Colonel Sellers in *The Gilded Age,* who could always see "millions in it,"

Almost any promoter who came to him with a

new invention could be certain that Sam would make a sizable investment. He squandered $32,000 on the development of a power pulley which never succeeded in pulling anything, except more money from his pocket. He invested heavily in a steam generator which was supposed to recapture ninety per cent of the energy released in the burning of coal. Into a typesetting machine (infinitely alluring to a man who had spent nine years of his life setting type by hand) he eventually poured $190,000. Of all his business ventures only his publishing company seemed temporarily to be profitable. He sold several hundred thousand sets of General Grant's memoirs, paying Grant's widow one of the largest royalty checks on record. But even in this field, his years of success were numbered.

However, we are talking now of the days before disaster struck—the golden era between 1870 and 1885 when most of his finest books were written, when the three daughters were growing up—when Quarry Farm furnished a creative vacation every summer, and the great house in Hartford was the scene of solid comfort and friendship throughout the rest of the year.

Sometimes, of course, he was away lecturing—which Livy dreaded, and Sam endured with fortitude. But one journey from home he thoroughly enjoyed. This was in the spring of 1882 when he made the round trip from St. Louis to New Orleans by steamboat, standing many watches at the wheel. The return voyage was made with his old friend and teacher Horace Bixby. The beauty of the great mid-continent stream overwhelmed him again as it lay before him, in sunlight and moonlight—coursing its regal way to the Gulf of Mexico, through chutes and over bars, oxbowing around whole counties of fertile soil.

While in the Middle West, Sam visited St. Louis, talking wistfully of the early days. In Hannibal he chatted for long hours with friends of his youth. The deep and winding cave, the magic island, and Holliday's Hill were much as he had remembered them.

Rested, refreshed, and reinspired, Sam returned to Hartford. The notes he had made during his weeks on the river furnished the needed material to complete his new book, *Life on the Mississippi*. And his visit to his boyhood home encouraged him to take up again a story long upon the shelf—his acknowledged masterpiece, *The Adventures of Huckleberry Finn.*

Upon rejoining his family, Mark Twain frequently discovered some delightful surprise prepared for him by Susy, Clara, Jean, and Livy. At about this time Susy and Clara wrote many plays, which they produced with the help of other children in the neighborhood. The audience often numbered ninety or one hundred friends, neighbors, and servants.

Susy believed that, of all her father's books, *The Prince and the Pauper* was the finest; and this she had elaborately dramatized during his absence. Costumes, sets, and directing had been supervised in Susy's usual competent manner. All three of the Clemens girls had parts in the play, even four-year-old Jean, who performed her role beautifully. She sat at a desk writing out death warrants, beaming happily. Sometimes, in a lull between warrants, she put her head on the desk and quietly went to sleep (it was considerably past her bedtime).

Mark Twain was moved by this sensitive dramatization of his book. But within a few months he was even more deeply moved by another product of Susy's pen. It was a biography of her father which she had been writing secretly.

"We are a very happy family. We consist of Papa, Mamma, Jean, Clara and me. It is papa I am writing about . . . he is a *very* striking character.

"Papa's appearance has been described many times, but very incorrectly. He has beautiful gray hair, not any too thick or any too long, but just right; a Roman nose, which greatly improves the beauty of his features; kind blue eyes and a small mustache. He has a wonderfully shaped head and profile. He has a very good figure—in short he is an extraordinarily fine looking man . . . He is a very good man and a very funny one. He *has* got a temper, but we all of us have in this family. He is the loveliest man I ever saw or ever hope to see—and oh, so absent-minded. He does tell perfectly delightful stories."

Mark Twain would receive many glowing eulogies during his remaining years, but not one which he would treasure as he did the few pages Susy wrote. His "slender little maid with plaited tails of copper-tinged hair down her back"—the girl who would so soon lie dead—had paid him the ultimate tribute.

8

THE LONG JOURNEY
HOME
(1885–1910)

It would be pleasant to leave Clemens and his "very happy family" as they were in November 1885 when he celebrated his fiftieth birthday. Dr. Oliver Wendell Holmes sent verses commemorating the event. Letters and thoughtful gifts arrived from the four corners of the earth, some merely addressed to "Mark Twain, America"! All arrived safely. Surrounded by his loving family, friends, and neighbors —successful, famous, and free from debt—this still vital and productive author seemed blessed by the gods of Mount Olympus.

However, shadows were already gathering to dim this picture. Business worries were beginning to sap the creative energy which should have been channeled into his writing. His publishing company was struggling for existence, and royalties from his books soon began to dwindle. In the spring of 1891 it was apparent to Sam and Livy that they could no longer maintain their mansion in Hartford, and in June of that year they closed the big house forever to begin nine years of economical wandering through Europe.

In the year 1894, Twain's publishing company failed, leaving him with a staggering debt of $70,000, incurred by his incompetent partner. He vowed to pay every cent of this obligation, and in a little less than five years managed to do so.

Twain at this time was himself both a prince and a pauper. He was bankrupt, but the toast of every monarch he met and every country in which he lived. His world-wide lecture tour in 1895 and 1896 was like a royal procession, westward across America and across the Pacific to New Zealand, Australia, India, Ceylon, and South Africa; northward to England; then, grief-stricken, back to America again, to bury his beloved Susy, who in the last days of her parents' absence had died of spinal meningitis.

For eight years after Susy's death, Sam neither played the piano nor sang the spirituals which had moved him so profoundly since the days of his childhood. Something irreplaceable had vanished from his life. But now on a June evening of 1904 in Florence, Italy, there was again a song in his heart.

Olivia had been seriously ill for twenty-two months, often so near to death that Sam was not allowed to enter her room, but only to hover outside her door writing little letters sent in to cheer her. On this particular day, however, she had seemed more nearly her former spirited self. Sam had been allowed to eat dinner with her, and they had talked of their good life together for more than an hour. He had left her reluctantly at last, pausing at the door to throw her a kiss, and promising to be back at nine-thirty to say good night.

Sam mounted the marble stairs of the old palace in which they were living, and in the room above went to the piano and began playing and singing softly:

Swing low, sweet chariot,
Coming for to carry me home . . .

In her chamber below, Livy said dreamily, "He is singing a good-night carol to me." And so he was, for in another few minutes she was dead.

Sam brought her home to America. It was their last journey together. She was buried from the same parlors of her girlhood home in which she had stood as a bride thirty-four years before. She would sleep now in the family plot in Elmira beside her little son Langdon and her daughter Susy. Sam stood bewildered at these graves, the wind ruffling his white hair. Slowly he read the verse he had placed on Susy's stone, four lines which now applied to Livy too:

> *Warm summer sun, shine kindly here;*
> *Warm southern wind, blow softly here;*
> *Green sod above, lie light, lie light!—*
> *Good night, dear heart, good night,*
>   *good night.*

Organ music from his great orchestrelle became the principal solace of the bereft Mark Twain during his six remaining years—symphonic music now, Beethoven, Schubert, and Chopin. Because he could not bear the thought of black—reminding him of death—he dressed in white from head to foot—his hair and flowing mustache as snowy as his clothes. Sometimes he "wore a white kitten" on his shoulder, fondling it idly. Often he played a contemplative game of billiards, sending the white balls across their little field of green. Propped up against the white pillows of his enormous bed, he wrote on endless pages of white paper—almost never completing a manuscript.

Honors continued to come his way, but most of them meant little to him. For an evening he was cheered by his seventieth-birthday banquet at Delmonico's in New York. At Oxford he wore his gray and crimson cap and gown with distinction, and was moved by the response of the audience when he received his honorary doctorate of letters. Affectionate laughter and unashamed tears greeted each rare appearance of this handsome old humorist, the most famous, the most beloved, and, in some ways, the most tragic literary figure of his era.

No possible sorrow was to be spared him in those closing years. At Stormfield, his new home near Redding, Connecticut, his daughter Jean had decorated the Christmas tree and wrapped dozens of gifts. Jean was the comfort of Mark Twain's old age, working beyond her strength to manage the estate, keep the financial records and serve as secretary to her father. He begged her to spare herself —but Jean was both devoted and determined— cheerful now as she added the last touches to what would surely be their best Christmas in years.

Then on the morning of December 24th, 1909, Jean Clemens was found dead in her bath—the victim of an epileptic stroke.

Sam Clemens had said that he would never again listen to clods of earth being dropped on the coffin of one he loved. Faithful Katy Leary, their servant since the children were babies, accompanied Jean's body to Elmira. Sam stood bare-headed in the door of his home—the Christmas decorations behind him, the desolate world of swirling snow outside—watching the hearse move slowly down the drive.

How very little either his money or fame could buy! Not one more hour of Susy's life, or Livy's or Jean's. But soon, he hoped, he would join them in Elmira. He had arrived with Halley's comet in 1835. He had always said that he would make his departure with its predicted return in 1910. Promptly on schedule that flaming astral body swept into the sky from its mysterious journey through outer space. Mark Twain was ready for the rendezvous. He slipped away peacefully just as the sun was setting on April 21st, 1910.

In a greater sense, however, Mark Twain still lives for every reader who discovers Tom Sawyer and Huckleberry Finn. And there are many of us who believe that he will continue to live while "the majestic, the magnificent Mississippi" rolls its "mile-wide tide along."

INDEX